# THE BLOODAXE BOOK OF
## CONTEMPORARY
# WOMEN POETS
### Eleven British Writers
## EDITED BY JENI COUZYN

# BLOODAXE BOOKS

ISBN: 0 906427 79 7 hardback
      0 906427 80 0 paperback

First published 1985 by
Bloodaxe Books Ltd,
P.O. Box 1SN,
Newcastle upon Tyne NE99 1SN.


Bloodaxe Books Ltd acknowledges
the financial assistance of Northern Arts.


Second impression 1985
Third impression 1987
Fourth impression 1989
Fifth impression 1990.


Typesetting by True North, Newcastle upon Tyne.

Printed in Great Britain by Bell and Bain Ltd., Glasgow

*For Veda and Geordie*

# CONTENTS

## RUTH FAINLIGHT (born 1931)

## SYLVIA PLATH (1932-1963)

## JENNY JOSEPH (born 1932)

## ANNE STEVENSON (born 1933)

## FLEUR ADCOCK (born 1934)

## JENI COUZYN (born 1942)

The reciter said: These, my dear one, were the words of the womb-woman, and lovely, methinks, was her language, and beautiful it was to hear her. O Mary of grace, many a beautiful thing had the people who are gone, though it is not much of these that can be gleaned today. No, my dear one, they do not exist. The gentle Christian folk are gone who took an interest in the old things, good and venerable, of their country. I remember myself, though I was little at the time, when the Christian folk crowded into one another's houses, telling tales and histories, invocations and prayers, singing hymns and songs, runes and lays, sweet, beautiful and soft. Many a goodly thing there was – O many a goodly thing there was among the old people who are gone. The good people of that day lived not on senseless babbling – no my dear one, they disdained gossip and scandal. The old people conversed about the state of the world and about the changes of the weather, about the moon and the sun, about the stars of the sky, about the ebbing and flowing of the sea, about life in the depths of the ocean, and about the hot and the cold lands of the earth. We children would be sitting on the bare flat of the floor, not uttering a syllable, nor moving a hand, lest we should be put out of the house were we not mannerly. O King! 'tis there would be the talk! – and noble talk.

You can hear nothing of that today, goodwife, said I.

No, my dear, no, it does not exist. The dear Christian folk who gave heed to it are beyond the river, where I myself shall shortly be. O Mary of grace, mayest thou give me thy two arms around mine everlasting soul when going over the black river of death whither my beloved have gone to rest!

The wife of Donald, son of Eoghan, crofter, Barra [*Carmina Gadelica/Ortha nan Gaidheal*, 6 vols (Scottish Academic Press, Edinburgh, 1900-71), III].

# Introduction

Poetry in Britain has not always been dominated by men, as Shakespeare acknowledged in *Twelfth Night*:

> The spinsters, and the knitters in the sun,
> And the free maids that weave their thread with bones,
> Do use to chant it.

The Gaelic traditional poetry of the Scottish Highlands is one of the great oral traditions of the world. We owe its survival as literature partly to the life's work of one dedicated family – Elizabeth Carmichael (Watson), her father Alexander Carmichael, her mother Mary Carmichael, and her son J. Watson Carmichael. In their six-volume collection the greater proportion of reciters were women, and it seems both from the content of the poems and Alexander Carmichael's explanations of them that they were made by women and handed down from mother to daughter. They are a collection of work songs, healing charms, stories and prayers and spells, woven into the essential texture of the lives of those who spoke them, and tell of a society radically different from ours. Theirs was a society where people lived in harmony with the earth based on a deep respect and love for all things living. They invoked their spiritual power to help them in their daily lives as naturally and effectively as we invoke the power of machinery. Poetry was the means by which they projected their inner power – poems sung, spoken, handed down, and kept alive for generations.

Carmichael wrote of the Highland people in his introduction to the *Carmina Gadelica* in 1899:

> Mirth and music, song and dance, tale and poem, pervaded their lives, as electricity pervades the air. Religion, pagan or Christian, or both combined, permeated everything – blending and shading into one another like the iridescent colours of the rainbow. The people were sympathetic and synthetic, unable to see and careless to know where the secular began and the religious ended – an admirable union of elements in life for those who have lived it so truly and intensely as the Celtic races everywhere have done.

I was introduced to this great body of literature by Kathleen Raine, one of the first women poets to influence me. I met her in the late sixties, and found in her work a spiritual and lyrical power that was lacking in most of the poetry then being praised in the national newspapers. Feeling herself firmly within the stream of 'true poetry', Raine has steadfastly refused to be drawn into the spiritually impoverished cul-de-sac of "clever" poetry that has dominated literary fashion in Britain for most of her writing life. Consequently, Raine has been much undervalued as a poet.

As a student in 1960, I was offered John Hayward's *Faber Book of English Verse* as a basic poetry text, an outline geography of the world of poetry. At the time, I didn't notice that poems by women fill only eleven of its four hundred and sixty-two pages.

When I came across the seventeenth-century poet Aphra Behn years later, I turned to the Faber book to see why I hadn't been interested in her work earlier. She's not in it. Nor is Elizabeth Barrett Browning, Anne Bradstreet, Ruth Pitter, Alice Meynell, Charlotte Mew, Laura Riding, Hilda Doolittle, Katherine Phillips, Amy Lowell, Edna St Vincent Millay, Vita Sackville-West, Dorothy Parker, Louise Bogan . . . . at first in ones and twos, then in a mounting tide, women poets began to flow into that moon-dry sea bed of my heritage.

In America, poets and academics have been re-thinking the history of English poetry for several decades now, and the missing women poets have begun to take their places in it. But in Britain the tradition that women do not write great poetry is too unconscious and too deep to be easily shifted, even when superficial changes in attitude appear to be occurring.

In his preface to the Faber book, Hayward thanked Miss Kathleen Raine and Miss Helen Gardner for their advice. In the *New Oxford Book of English Verse* (1972) the latter, now Dame Helen Gardner, Emeritus Professor of English at Oxford, is the *editor*, and Raine actually has one small poem included. Otherwise, the book is not much changed from its predecessors. Of its eight hundred and eighty-four poems, twenty-nine are by women. The choice of women poets is well-meaning, but not well informed, and the content of their poems is restricted, on the whole, to the two subjects considered permissible for women poets in the nineteenth century: love and religion.

In 1980, Oxford brought out a companion anthology also intended as a university text: *The Oxford Book of Contemporary Verse, 1945-1980*, edited by D.J. Enright. This is an accurate account of the poetry in Britain which was fashionable during the period, but it leaves out the mass of poetry written by women. It has been an age of intellectual respectability, anxious to avoid 'the shrill and the hysterical' where freshness of language and the startling image have eclipsed all other virtues – a recipe, as David Daiches points out in his four-volume *Critical History of English Literature*, for good minor poetry. Of the forty poets Enright includes in his 1979 selection, three are women. They are: Patricia Beer, a favourite in the sixties and seventies for token woman, because she can be relied on never to embarrass the reader with anything too "female"; Elizabeth Bishop who, though almost unknown in her lifetime in Britain, received a flurry of attention at the time of her death in 1979; and Stevie Smith. Smith was never treated as a "serious" poet until her death in 1971 (although she was much loved by audiences at poetry readings), and her reputation reached a peak in 1979 after the wide acclaim Glenda Jackson received starring in the film *Stevie*.

In the absence of real respect for the work of women poets, the choice of token woman is subject to the fickle drifts of whim and fashion in any year, and the editors always admire the women poets they choose at the expense of all other women poets, justifying their choice with a sneer at women poets in general. A. Alvarez's praise for Plath's first book is typical: 'She steers clear of feminine charm, deliciousness, gentility, supersensitivity, and the act of being a poetess.'

We have three basic stereotypes of the woman poet, who is generally considered a rare and rather inferior sub-species of the genus Great Poet.

The first and most popular of these is *Mrs Dedication*, best personified by the myth of Elizabeth Barrett Browning. (The Real Barrett Browning had little to do with her popular image.) This poet directs all mental and emotional energy into romantic devotion to a man. She is necessarily beautiful and faithful, and if she can be fragile and die young as well, so much the better for her image. A love poem or two from her will be found in most anthologies.

The second and more common of the species is *Miss Eccentric Spinster*, personified by such poets as Emily Dickinson, pale in her white dress behind closed doors; Edith Sitwell, raucous and purple-cloaked; Stevie Smith nervy in tweed skirt and ankle socks on the stage of the Festival Hall. This version of the woman poet is generally considered to have been the victim of an unhappy love affair from which she never recovered. That she should have chosen not to marry, even, in some cases, chosen instead to direct her love towards women rather than men is seldom considered by her historians. *Spinster* implies that she has failed at the central task of her life, and in order to make her seem more interesting the notion of eccentricity is added to her image.

The third and most contemporary image for the woman poet is *Mad Girl* – the tormented life and early suicide. Sylvia Plath is the most celebrated of this group of poets.

A handful of poems by the woman poet is usually included in anthologies, but it's impossible to get a sensible picture of who the women poets are by looking through their contents lists. A sixth of the poems in the *Penguin Book of Contemporary British Poetry* (1982) were written by women (five women out of twenty poets), and Carcanet's rival 1983 selection contained none of the same women but two others (two out of eighteen poets). Not one of these seven appears in the *Penguin Book of Women Poets* (1978), where a quite different posy of names is supposed to represent contemporary women.

It has been suggested that the proportion of women poets is so low in comparison with the men because fewer women write poetry. A glance at one of the anthologies from the little presses, such as Peter Forbes's *A Poet's 1982* or Howard Sergeant's *Outposts* series of pamphlets, which draw their material mainly from magazines, makes it clear that this is not the case. In her anthology *Salt and Bitter and Good* Cora Kaplan quotes from an essay by the poet Theodore Roethke which illustrates male prejudice so vividly that I cannot resist repeating it here:

> Two of the charges most frequently levelled against poetry by women are lack of range – in subject matter, in emotional tone – and lack of sense of humour. And one could, in individual instances among writers of real talent, add other aesthetic and moral shortcomings: the spinning out; the embroidering of trivial themes; a concern with the mere surfaces of life – that special province of the feminine talent in prose – hiding from the real agonies of the spirit; refusing to face up to what existence is, lyric or religious posturing; running between the boudoir and the altar, stamping a tiny foot against God; or lapsing into a sententiousness that implies the author has re-invented integrity; carrying on excessively about Fate, about time; lamenting the lot of women; caterwauling; writing the same poem about fifty times, and so on.

Geoffrey Summerfield in his anthology *Worlds*, published by Penguin in 1974, insults women poets more briefly: 'I regret the omission of women poets from this book. This is simply due to the fact that Britain in the last fifteen years has not produced a woman poet of real stature.'

A literature that does not include the depth and range of female consciousness is bound to be an amputated one, and reflect back a dangerously distorted image of the society it is supposed to illuminate. Yet there have always been women poets of 'real stature'. Their survival has depended on extraordinary strength and determination. The most obvious difficulty they have had to overcome has been inferior education. Oxford and Cambridge universities are traditionally the most fertile breeding grounds for English poets. (Of the five poets in this anthology educated at English universities, all are Oxbridge graduates!) Yet even in 1978, only one in eight places were allocated to female students, and in 1985 it is still only one in three.

More difficult for women poets to overcome is the traditional attitude towards women's role in society. Although it comes in the wrapping of romantic love, and gives women status, marriage is the contract by which women poets sign away their right to work.

Rearing young children demands a mind that spreads itself outward like a wide and shallow lake, calm, generous and receptive, totally reliable. But writing poetry requires a mind rushing inwards to its centre like a silent, deep and narrow river, driven by its own direction. The poet needs to be ruthless, one-pointed, undistracted.

Not many of the great women poets have chosen to be, or to remain, wives (Emily Dickinson, Stevie Smith, Charlotte Mew, Edith Sitwell, Christina Rossetti, all remained unmarried). Those who do marry frequently marry other poets, confusing their passion for poetry itself with love for a man who can write it. Many women poets have broken their own hearts by abandoning their children, or in despair at reconciling the roles of wife/mother with that of poet, have taken their own lives.

As I lurched through my twenties, conscious of the many women poets I admired who had taken their own lives – Sylvia Plath, Anne Sexton, Ingrid Jonker, Eva Royston, Marina Tsvetayeva – I deeply believed that the choice for me was between "happiness" (i.e. home, husband, and children) or poetry. The consequence of choosing "happiness" would be losing the ability to write, and of choosing poetry would be an early suicide. This was not so much an idea as a tangible feeling within my life of the tug of opposing energies.

Yet the great men poets have often had dedicated wives who have served them all their lives, freeing them to serve "the Muse" without domestic or secretarial burdens, and many have had mistresses as well.

The lives of Virginia Woolf and the Brontës suggest a similar pattern among women novelists, though they have been less handicapped by male censorship because novels become popular by being read – and women read more novels than men do. Poetry on the other hand, is read for pleasure only by very few. It is mainly valued (by our society) as the castor oil of education – that which one "didn't much care for at school but was forced to learn", and no child would be considered educated in our society unless it had been forced to swallow some of the unpleasant stuff. It is considered good for growing minds, as milk is good for young bodies, but only the strangest mental athletes expect to go on taking it after they grow up.

Therefore, it is the educators, the critics, the academics and the editors and publishers who have given poets reputations and these are all male dominated, 'goblin-ridden', as Rossetti would say, professions. Louise Bernikow, in her introduction to *The World Split Open*, says that the context for a study of women's poetry is women's politics.

In the late sixties, a male friend of mine was commissioned by a publisher to edit an anthology of love poems by women and he passed the project to me. As I read the poems of contemporary women, I found that I was not alone in what I was writing, but surrounded by women poets who were all writing poems that were angry, powerful, hurt, tender, and defiant. I delighted in the unique female voice of Stevie Smith:

> Do take Muriel out
> Although your name is Death
> She will not complain
> When you dance her over the blasted heath . . .

the cool fury of Fleur Adcock in poems like 'Against Coupling', 'Advice to a Discarded Lover', and 'Instructions to Vampires':

> . . . use acid or flame,
> Secretly, to brand or cauterize;
> And on the soft globes of his mortal eyes
> Etch my name . . .

and especially the haunting loss in poems by Kathleen Raine like 'The Unloved':

> I am pure loneliness
> I am empty air
> I am drifting cloud.
>
> I have no form
> I am boundless
> I have no rest.

The anthology told a story I believed to be true – that men no longer loved women. It was a story of pain and courage and humour. The publisher was appalled at my choice (he'd had delicate lyrics in mind) and dropped the project.

But I went on reading the poems, feeling that I had been liberated. These women were writing, as *women*, poems that no man could possibly have written, and challenging the way we have defined ourselves in relation to men – as lovers, mothers, wives. Denise Levertov's poem 'The Mutes' is an important poem in any history of poetry, because it explores new territory for literature:

Those groans men use
passing a woman on the street
or on the steps of the subway

to tell her she is a female
and their flesh knows it,

are they a sort of tune,
an ugly enough song, sung
by a bird with a slit tongue

but meant for music?

Levertov wrote about love, as women poets are expected to, but she
wrote about it in a way that male values could not have charted for
her. She also wrote about marriage. In her poem 'The Ache of
Marriage' she says of it:

It is leviathan and we
in its belly
looking for joy, some joy
not to be known outside it

two by two in the ark of
the ache of it.

Such anguish! However joyless marriage might be – confined in an
ark or in the stomach of a whale – it is the only alternative to being
swallowed by the deep.

Anne Sexton's poems of the late sixties were also exploring new
ways for women to write poetry that had nothing to do with how
men expect women to feel. In her remarkable poem 'For My Lover
Returning to His Wife' the poet is outside the marriage ark, looking
inwards at the wife. The wife is both beloved and loving, endlessly
giving and endlessly forgiving – and therefore beautiful and desir-
able. Here though, the woman looking in at the wife is her husband's
mistress. The poem expresses all the yearning for that idealised role,
at the same time rejecting it. Sexton, like so many women poets,
rejected the role of wife after a time, knowing it as an impossible role
to reconcile with the demands of her inner voice. Yet the yearning for
that impossible dream is the life-fuse of this moving poem:

She is all there.
She was melted carefully down for you
and cast up from your childhood,
cast up from your one hundred favorite aggies.

She has always been there, my darling.
She is, in fact, exquisite.

Fireworks in the dull middle of February
and as real as a cast-iron pot.

Let's face it, I have been momentary.
A luxury. A bright red sloop in the harbor.
My hair rising like smoke from the car window.
Littleneck clams out of season.

She is more than that. She is your have to have,
has grown you your practical your tropical growth.
This is not an experiment. She is all harmony.
She sees to oars and oarlocks for the dinghy,

has placed wild flowers at the window at breakfast,
sat by the potter's wheel at midday,
set forth three children under the moon,
three cherubs drawn by Michelangelo,

done this with her legs spread out
in the terrible months in the chapel.
If you glance up, the children are there
like delicate balloons resting on the ceiling.

She has also carried each one down the hall
after supper, their heads privately bent,
two legs protesting, person to person,
her face flushed with a song and their little sleep.

I give you back your heart.
I give you permission —

for the fuse inside her, throbbing
angrily in the dirt, for the bitch in her
and the burying of her wound —
for the burying of her small red wound alive —

for the pale flickering flare under her ribs,
for the drunken sailor who waits in her left pulse,
for the mother's knee, for the stockings,
for the garter belt, for the call —

the curious call
when you will burrow in arms and breasts
and tug at the orange ribbon in her hair
and answer the call, the curious call.

She is so naked and singular.
She is the sum of yourself and your dream.
Climb her like a monument, step after step.
She is solid.

As for me, I am watercolor.
I wash off.

For me, reading Anne Sexton in 1969, when her *Love Poems* was first published in Britain, was a revelation, but neither *Love Poems* nor *Transformations* (equally exciting, published in 1971) was well received here, and her name did not begin to appear in British anthologies.

*How* women poets have been excluded from the central repertoire of English literature is a mystery currently being unravelled by academic women writers. *Why* they have been excluded is a more serious question. What is woman's consciousness, that man cannot stand it in the world he has made? One thing though is certain – it has always been for the *content*, and not the style or form of their work that men have disliked women's poetry.

Aphra Behn was dominant as a poet and playwright in the literary world of the seventeenth century. In her own time she was popular enough to make writing a serious profession, by which she earned her living, but subsequent critics found it distasteful for a woman to write about sex with such frankness and humour, so they rejected her work. Later, she was simply forgotten.

Characteristic of her poems is 'The Disappointment' where Behn turns her wit to satirise male fantasy at its most ridiculous. The amorous shepherd (all the rage in the seventeenth century) forces himself on a virgin, but instead of being victim, she responds with enthusiasm. Her eagerness takes him by surprise, and with mounting rage, he discovers himself to be impotent. He is left smouldering with humiliation when she flees, convinced that his heartless attempt to seduce her was, naturally, all her fault:

> His silent Griefs swell up to storms
> And not one God his Fury spares;
> He curs'd his Birth, his Fate, his Stars;
> But more the Shepherdess's Charms,
> Whose soft bewitching influence
> Had damn'd him to the hell of impotence.

Notice the use of 'bewitching' – as though her beauty were a creation of the black arts, specifically designed for his damnation. Behn is mocking him, and through him, all men. It's no wonder that male editors prefer to forget her!

Elizabeth Barrett Browning has been censored in subsequent ages by selective rather than complete omission – unlike Behn, she does appear in anthologies. She is often used as the "token" woman – the civilising influence of the gentler sex demure in a corner, and represented, appropriately, by love poems dedicated to her husband. Popular myth paints her as a beautiful and fragile invalid, wasting away in the house of a tyrannical father. Enter Robert Browning, the Prince of Poetry, who sweeps her away (at dead of night, of course) to Romantic Italy, where she miraculously recovers to enjoy fifteen magical years of love, and to publish her *Sonnets from the Portuguese*.

The reissue in 1978 of *Aurora Leigh*, with a fascinating introduction by Cora Kaplan, has done much to correct this image. Barrett Browning was a powerful influence in her time, far better known than her husband, Robert, and a serious candidate for poet laureate after Wordsworth's death in 1850. She wrote a large body of work, much of it political. She was an active and militant feminist, deeply committed to social reform. The suffering of the poor, child labour, the constrictions on women's lives, and the abolition of slavery, were all subjects for her poems.

*Aurora Leigh* is an epic novel-length poem that ran through thirteen editions in the sixteen years following its publication in 1853. It was thoroughly and extensively reviewed, heralded by Ruskin as 'the first perfect poetical expression of the age', and read by everyone in polite society including the Queen.

Some of the themes Barrett Browning explores in *Aurora Leigh* are set out in the prologue to her poem, 'A Curse for a Nation'. The poet is instructed by an angel to write a curse on America because of its system of slavery. The angel represents Barrett Browning's higher self – her Daemon, or Muse. The injunction is that she should write a *curse* – that she should draw on anger that is clean and pure – the flaming-sword, angelic anger that comes from love of justice and truth, not to be confused with the cloying anger of emotion:

> From the summits of love a curse is driven,
> As lightning is from the tops of heaven.

Barrett Browning is acknowledging herself as real woman – not the simpering weakling who dissolves in tears at the slightest provocation, but woman who is daughter of the Goddess Kali, destroyer of all that is false. It is precisely because she loves truth enough to turn the full beam of her consciousness to gaze within that true woman is able to write the angel's curse:

> 'Therefore', the voice said, 'shalt thou write
>     My curse tonight.
> Because thou hast strength to see and hate
> A foul thing done *within* thy gate.'

Barrett Browning has little patience with the posturing of man-made woman who pretends to be too frail to undertake anything important:

'Not so', I answered once again.
   'To curse, choose men.
For I, a woman, have only known
How the heart melts and the tears run down'.

To which the angel replies:

'A curse from the depths of womanhood
Is very salt, and bitter, and good'.

It is from 'the depths of womanhood' that Barrett Browning draws her power – a power that transcends the personal not by ignoring but by examining the idea of woman presented to her by Victorian society.

Barrett Browning chose her friends from feminists and reformers, but saw all around her women like her mother who bore eleven children and suffered her husband's tyranny with meekness and passivity.

It is with the angel's curse that Barrett Browning attacked the social injustices of her time:

'My heart is sore
For my own land's sins: for little feet
Of children bleeding along the street:

For parked up honours that gainsay
   The right of way!
For almsgiving through a door that is
Not open enough for two friends to kiss!

For love of freedom which abates
   Beyond the Straits:
For patriot virtue starved to vice on
Self praise, self-interest, and suspicion'.

When Barrett Browning died in 1861, England mourned the loss of one of its leading literary figures, yet in the twentieth-century "revision" of the canons of English literature, as Kaplan calls it, her place was left empty.

Another major poet whose work was not to the taste of subsequent male critics was Christina Rossetti. A key to her work is 'Goblin Market', the title poem of her first book, published when she was thirty-one. It's an immature work with the flawed beauty of a great poet in need of an editor – a few stern pencil strokes would have sufficed. Rossetti's later work is less uneven than 'Goblin Market', yet in spite of its flaws, it is one of her most evocative and haunting poems. It masquerades as a poem for children about goblins and virgins, but bursts its seams in every stanza, and undoubtedly draws its power from a deeply personal account of love and danger.

The central theme of the poem is the innocent but sensual love of two adolescent sisters for each other, and their subsequent awakening. It works at an allegorical level – the sisters drawn in images of childlike purity – doves, lilies, new fallen snow, and male sexuality represented by devilish goblin merchants, endlessly cunning and malevolent. These creatures hawk their magical but deadly fruit to each young girl once only, then, their harm accomplished, slither back into the crevices of the earth.

Mortal men, with kindly human feelings, are completely absent from this poem. It could be described as a kind of Fall-from-Eden tale where male sexuality is the apple that poisons female love and brings about the loss of paradise.

The story begins with the sisters lying close in each other's arms, with 'tingling cheeks and fingertips' cautioning each other not to peep at the goblin men as they troop by. Laura can barely stand the sight of their fruit, and begins to sigh:

> 'How fair the vine must grow
> Whose grapes are so luscious;
> How warm the wind must blow
> Through those fruit bushes.'

The temptation proves too much for her and she succumbs to the goblin feast. Thereafter, she is doomed, becoming more cankerous and listless with each passing day. Her life is saved by her sister who subjects herself to a fairy-tale version of rape by the goblins which results in an intense but final sexual encounter between the two girls. Lizzie arrives home crying:

> 'Never mind my bruises,
> Hug me, kiss me, suck my juices,
> Squeezed from goblin fruits for you,
> Goblin pulp and goblin dew.
> Eat me, drink me, love me . . .'

But as Laura turns hungrily towards her:

> Her lips began to scorch,
> That juice was wormwood to her tongue . . .
> She gorged on bitterness without a name . . .

Laura becomes the battleground of a collision between good and evil presented in images of stricken towers, earthquake, lightning and sea-storm. Good is represented by her sister's love, and evil by male sexuality. When she recovers from this ordeal, Laura hugs Lizzie, 'but not twice or thrice'. Rossetti, complying with the morals of her time, is suggesting that homosexual love, while innocent in adolescents, is no longer acceptable in grown women. But her heart told her otherwise, and her later work is tormented by the split between goodness *believed in* and goodness *felt*. Self-negation and a sense of loss permeate her later poems.

The poem is formally framed by the girls becoming 'wives' – something Rossetti never did – and she herself seems to lose interest in them. But the message of the poem is explicitly restated in the final stanza, where mothers warn their daughters that male sexuality stirs up passions that are 'honey to the throat/but poison in the blood' whereas love between sisters can be passionate, tender and heroic.

When he edited her collected poems, it is significant that her brother William Michael Rossetti extracted from the work half a dozen poems which, from their titles, appear to have been love poems addressed directly to women.

Emily Dickinson, born in the same year as Rossetti, but on the other side of the Atlantic, was an admirer of Elizabeth Barrett Browning and greatly influenced by her. But where Barrett Browning was public, Dickinson was private; where Barrett Browning looked outward at the world, Dickinson looked inward into her own soul; where Barrett Browning sought to change the suffering in the world by challenging it, Dickinson sought to transmute it by enduring, and passing through it. Both poets were feminists, but Barrett Browning's feminism was articulated and intellectualised, whereas Dickinson's feminism was *lived* – she chose to express her own life without defining herself in relation to a set of male values, or by seeking male approval, either in love or in her work.

Dickinson is one of the greatest poets in the English language. Only seven of her poems were published in her own lifetime. But she wrote nearly two thousand, and it was only after her death in 1886 that these were discovered in a chest in her bedroom. It took another seventy years for all the poems to be published as she'd written them. (Meddling editors couldn't accept her uniqueness, and tried to improve on the poems.)

Male critics have painted Dickinson as a half-cracked little spinster for many decades. And her biographers have searched endlessly through her acquaintances for a great lost love. The role of wife would soon have gagged and eroded the poet in her, so she chose not to marry or squander her energy in romantic involvement. What she sought above all was union with her own soul, a union she expressed through her poems, and at times embodied as the beloved. Much of her work is an account of the journey into that private territory. The first gateway is a loneliness so horrifying that simply to confront it

could destroy one. Yet the poet enters, certain that within its corridors is the celestial light. And always beside the light is danger that
those corridors could seal her in forever.

> The Loneliness One dare not sound –
> And would as soon surmise
> As in its Grave go plumbing
> To ascertain the size –
>
> The Loneliness whose worst alarm
> Is lest itself should see –
> And perish from before itself
> For just a scrutiny –
>
> The Horror not to be surveyed –
> But skirted in the Dark –
> With Consciousness suspended –
> And Being under Lock –
>
> I fear me this – is Loneliness –
> The Maker of the soul
> Its Caverns and its Corridors
> Illuminate – or seal –

Beyond the the caverns of loneliness is a state of despair, where the
only feeling is a sensation of numbness. Madness at one elbow,
suicide at the other, chaos at one's feet and all around – many poets
have lost their footing here, yet Dickinson chose to endure this pain
again and again for the quality of life she knew to be beyond it. That
she could write poems of this quality from the depths of such pain is a
measure of her genius.

> It was not Death, for I stood up,
> And all the Dead, lie down –
> It was not Night, for all the Bells
> Put out their Tongues, for Noon.
>
> It was not Frost, for on my Flesh
> I felt Siroccos – crawl –
> Nor Fire – for just my Marble feet
> Could keep a Chancel, cool –
>
> And yet, it tasted, like them all,
> The Figures I have seen
> Set orderly, for Burial,
> Reminded me, of mine –
>
> As if my life were shaven,
> And fitted to a frame,
> And could not breathe without a key,
> And 'twas like Midnight, some –

When everything that ticked – has stopped –
And Space stares all around –
Or Grisly frosts – first Autumn morns,
Repeal the Beating Ground –

But, most, like Chaos – Stopless – cool –
Without a Chance, or Spar –
Or even a Report of Land –
To justify – Despair.

Surely this is the nadir of spiritual agony, yet Dickinson goes on, deeper, and deeper, her ability to record not faltering by so much as a syllable:

After great pain, a formal feeling comes –
The Nerves sit ceremonious, like Tombs –
The stiff Heart questions was it He, that bore,
And Yesterday, or Centuries before?

The Feet, mechanical, go round –
Of Ground, or Air, or Ought –
A Wooden way
Regardless grown,
A Quartz contentment, like a stone –

This is the Hour of Lead –
Remembered, if outlived,
As Freezing persons, recollect the Snow –
First – Chill – then Stupor – then the letting go –

Beyond the letting go is death, and beyond death is the encounter with the Daemon. Dickinson's final triumph is an affirmation of herself as fully realised. This poem is a celebration of the coming to consciousness, and taking of full responsibility for what one is. It is the triumphal entry of the *Being* into the *person*.

I'm ceded – I've stopped being Theirs –
The name They dropped upon my face
With water, in the country church
Is finished using, now,
And They can put it with my Dolls,
My childhood, and the string of spools,
I've finished threading – too –

Baptized, before, without the choice,
But this time, consciously, of Grace –
Unto supremest name –
Called to my Full – the Crescent dropped –
Existence's whole Arc, filled up,
With one small Diadem.

My second Rank – too small the first –
Crowned – Crowing – on my Father's breast –
A half unconscious Queen –
But this time – Adequate – Erect,
With Will to choose, or to reject,
And I choose, just a Crown –

Perhaps Emily Dickinson opened the way for the deluge of excellent women poets, critics, editors and academics that has completely changed the face of North American literature in this century, and which is at last beginning to cause small ripples here.

Two fine anthologies have been published: Louise Bernikow's *The World Split Open*, first published in America in 1974, was republished in Britain by The Women's Press in 1979. *Salt and Bitter and Good*, edited by Cora Kaplan, was published by Paddington Press in Britain. Penguin, vaguely sensing a gap and deciding to cash in on it, brought out a collection called *Women Poets* that spans forty different cultures and three and a half thousand years in one small volume. Its editors are aware of the impossibility of their task, and one must blame the publishers for this insulting and ludicrous book.

But in other parts of the world poetry by women is thriving. In Canada the poets P.K. Page, Gwendolyn MacEwen, Dorothy Livesay, Margaret Atwood, Phyllis Webb, and many younger poets receive as much and probably more acclaim than their male colleagues. I have been nourished by their work in recent years, as I have by the Russian poets Anna Akhmatova (translated by D.M. Thomas), and Marina Tsvetayeva, rendered into wonderful English poems by the poet Elaine Feinstein. In Russia poetry has long occupied a place of honour and power, and in contemporary Russian society women poets have been as much persecuted by the state for their poems as men have. In such a dangerous climate, it would seem that sexual prejudice has found no place among the great writers.

My aim in this anthology was to present generous selections from the work of just eleven British poets. They are all either British-born or have lived and worked in Britain. Those born elsewhere (Sylvia Plath, Anne Stevenson, Fleur Adcock, Ruth Fainlight and myself) established their reputations in Britain while living here. I have also restricted the anthology to the older generation of women poets (they are all over 40). I have included poets whose work is particularly close to me, and who have published at least four or five books. I trust that this anthology will encourage editors to celebrate and circulate the work of the many other contemporary women poets I admire.

I am grateful to Neil Astley for making it possible for this book to work its way out into the light, to Diana Reich and Frankie Finn for helping me over the last hump and to my daughter Tarot whose presence has anchored me in love from the moment she was born.

JENI COUZYN

# STEVIE SMITH

**Stevie Smith** was born Florence Margaret Smith in Hull in 1902. When she was three she moved to live with her mother and sister at her aunt's house in Palmers Green, London, which became her home for the rest of her life. She was educated at Palmers Green High School and the North London Collegiate School for Girls. She worked in a publisher's office until 1953, when she retired to look after her aunt. In 1971 she died of a brain tumour.

Stevie Smith's three novels, *Novel on Yellow Paper* (1936), *Over the Frontier* (1938) and *The Holiday* (1949) have recently been reissued by Virago. She published ten books of poems, including a *Selected Poems* in 1962 and the posthumous *Scorpion* in 1972. In 1975 her *Collected Poems* appeared from Allen Lane, and in 1978 a Penguin *Selected Poems* edited by James MacGibbon. Also available are *Me Again: Uncollected Writings of Stevie Smith*, edited by Jack Barbera and William McBrien (Virago, 1981), and *Stevie Smith: A Selection*, edited by Hermione Lee (Faber, 1983).

# Stevie Smith by JENI COUZYN

Of the house in North London where she lived from her fourth birthday until her death at sixty-eight, Stevie Smith has written:

It was a house of female habitation,
Two ladies fair inhabited the house,
And they were brave. For although Fear knocked loud
Upon the door, and said he must come in,
They did not let him in.
                                    ('A House of Mercy')

Her father was in the shipping business, and when the family firm collapsed under his mismanagement of it, he ran away to sea, leaving his wife to cope with their two small daughters. Both children were seriously ill throughout early childhood (Stevie Smith spent three years in hospital with TB from the age of five), and their mother was ill herself. However she made a safe home with her sister for her two daughters, and when her husband came home on twenty-four hours leave from time to time 'to borrow back/her Naval Officer's Wife's Allowance' she 'gave it him at once, she thought she should'.

Stevie Smith's memories of her father's brief visits home are always anti-heroic:

My mother was immensely loyal; no word was ever said against this creature, and appearances were kept up. He was very sentimental, the poor old thing, so we'd have to come down from bed, and I had to sit on his knee, you know, and be affectionate to the poor old darling, and I used to think, 'Twenty-four hours leave. I think I can stand it. It's expected of one. It's the least I can do, there's poor Daddy up in the snow and ice off Iceland.' He was on this Northern patrol a lot of the time, a very nasty patrol. I couldn't myself have been very fond of a man like that, because fundamentally he was a bore, as all very egotistical selfish people are bores.

Stevie Smith's mother and her aunt were the heroes of her childhood. She remembers them as two 'terribly sheltered and innocent ladies' who never had much money but who were courageous and sensible and unfailing. Her mother died when she was sixteen, and later her sister went away, but she lived on with her beloved aunt until she died (Smith died three years after her aunt).

Now I am old I tend my mother's sister
The noble aunt who so long tended us,
Faithful and True her name is. Tranquil.
Also Sardonic. And I tend the house.

It is a house of female habitation
A house expecting strength as it is strong
A house of aristocratic mould that looks apart
When tears fall; counts despair
Derisory. Yet it has kept us well. For all its faults,
If they are faults, of sternness and reserve,
It is a Being of warmth I think; at heart
A house of mercy.

                    ('A House of Mercy')

Neither Smith nor her aunt ever wished to marry. The aunt considered men 'very soppy individuals' and Smith, although she loved to have men for friends, would marvel at the way married women centred their lives round their husbands' needs and whims, even if they 'hated 'em like hell'. She thought marriage would be exhausting (she suffered all her life from a feeling of tiredness) and she explained her difference from other women as the result of her early conditioning:

> Most women . . . are conditioned early to having father the centre of home life, with father's chair, and father's dinner, and father's Times and father says, so they are not brought up like me to be this wicked selfish creature, to have no boring old father-talk, to have no papa at all that one attends to, to have a darling Aunt to come home to, that one admires, that is strong, happy, simple, shrewd, staunch, loving, upright and bossy, to have a darling sister that is working away from home, and to be for my Aunt, with this sister, the one.
>
> When I was getting too much the tyrant when I was a child, too domineering and too spoilt, because of being the youngest and because of being ill, when I was this over-bearing invalidish creature, this objectionable baby-boss, the worst that my gentle relatives would do to me was this, they would call me 'Miss Baby'. That cut the ground from under my imperious stamping feet, that shredded the imperial purple of my infant rage . . . Then the loving hands would lift me up, and everything was now over, and quite all right.

If Smith's mother and aunt lived sheltered lives, hers was even more sheltered. She never thought seriously of changing houses, or changing the known comfort of life with her aunt whom she dearly loved for the hazards of a life with someone else. In the same way, after she had gone from secretarial school into a job as a private secretary in a publishing firm, she never considered changing jobs, and worked in her first and only job until her retirement, when she took on some freelance journalism.

Her life was fired by a lively tension between opposites, the priorities of her dangerous internal and safe external landscapes. She lived on an edge of extreme anxiety – the kind of electric nervousness that comes from acute sensitivity and shyness, but that never dulled her quick ironic eye or her relentless wit. Fear is a recurring theme in her poems, but rather than having the effect of paralysis, it rises through them as a source of power and energy, a kind of mad sanity that reveals the 'precipice below the garden wall', and 'behind the eyes of the loved one, the bottomless dark eyes of the flying owl'. She felt great contempt for fear, as courageous people often do: 'For I said, if you cry for fear you are an abject character.' In her dealings with people she coped with her nervousness by wearing it like a kind of absurd fancy-dress. (I'll never forget my first sight of her, trembling like a frail bird on the stage of the Festival Hall, in her tweed skirt and ankle socks.) She played the part of the eccentric nervous spinster because it gave her a form in which to be courageous. And she wrote about fear with a kind of mad laughter:

> Harold was always afraid to climb high,
> But something urged him on,
> He felt he should try.
> I would not say he was wrong,
> Although he succeeded in doing nothing but die.
> Would you?
> Ever after that steep
> Place was called Harold's Leap.
> It was a brave thing to do.
>
> ('Harold's Leap')

Throughout her life, Smith had a running quarrel with God. She said of herself, 'I'm supposed to be an agnostic, but I'm sort of a backslider as a non-believer.' I get the feeling that she would have been more comfortable as a pantheist, but as in all things, she worked from within her given framework, so all her religious and philosophical energy addresses itself to a Christian god who comes in for much argument and comical criticism:

> I made Man with too many faults. Yet I love him.
> And if he wishes, I have a home above for him.
> I should like him to be happy. I am genial.
> He should not paint me as if I were abominable.
>
> ('God Speaks')

Perhaps her greatest quarrel with God is that he is a father figure, and Smith did not have a natural reverence for fathers:

> In the beginning, Father,
> You made the terms of our survival
> That we should use our intelligence
> To kill every rival.

The poison of this ferocity
Runs in our nature,
And O Lord thou knowest
How it nourishes thy creatures.
       ('Dear Child of God')

And so on. Her arguments are often convincing, usually amusing, and always poignant. At one of her rare moments of complete seriousness, when there is not also a smile lurking in the corner of her mouth, she writes:

> My uncle now began to storm and rave at me: You are blasphemous, spoilt, and evasive.
> No, Uncle, I am nervy, bold, and grim.

Her deep sadness was always for Smith a source of shame, and in her novel *The Holiday*, which is autobiographical as all her novels are, she talks it over with her aunt:

> For I want to know about this sadness defiency feeling. And I believe that some other people have it, but not my aunt, I should say not. But I believe that other people have it; and that at least is a consolation to bolster one up . . .
> I say, Was Mama a sad girl, Auntie, did Mama have these black-dog moods when she did not hate anybody so much as herself, and not the devil more?
> Your mother, said my Aunt was not a happy little girl, not so happy as she should have been.

'In some ways I'm romantic but my basic root is profoundly sensible,' Smith told her friend Kay Dick. On another occasion she said: 'It's better to be too lonely than too much with people you don't like.' However, it is from her romantic side that her loneliness and sadness were always generated. She regarded it as sensible to protect herself from the 'sudden dangerous capture made, made of oneself by a person who is outside . . . Ah then one gets scorched, then one is unhappy'. But she was always attracted by the 'wild laughing eyes' of the party guests, and 'Watch out, said Tommy, the word is Watchful.'

> Caz spoke in the most soft monotonous winning tones, my heart and the thoughts went out to the chinese distances.
> Oh Caz, I said, take me away, let me come with you, let me come with you on my pony, let me go away.
> Oh yes, said Caz, and what about the caliph and his son, eh, what about that? And to wander purposeless is to be a ghost . . .
> I looked at him in his eyes, it was the dark eyes of the flying owl.

Stevie Smith was very popular as a poet in her last few years, especially with young people, which she found difficult to understand as she saw her work as so melancholy and 'deathwards'. But at home she had what she regarded as the ideal for her work:

> My aunt used to say, 'I'm very glad you've got another book coming out but as you know I don't know much about it. It's all nonsense to me, my dear.' My aunt had a faintly sardonic attitude, I think, to the whole world.

Smith felt a loving antagonism to her muse:

> Who is this that howls and mutters?
> It is the Muse . . .
> > ('Who is this Who Howls and Mutters?')

> Dear Muse, the happy hours we have spent together.
> I love you so much in wet or fine weather.
> I only wish sometimes you would speak louder,
> But perhaps you will do so when you are prouder.
> I often think that this will be the next instant,
> Meanwhile I am your most obliging confidante.
> > ('Dear Muse')

How does Stevie Smith's strange doggerel poetry achieve its inimitable magic? This question is constantly asked both by her admirers and her critics, because she is an original voice in poetry with no back-up tradition and no imitators. "Eccentric" and "quirky" are words most frequently applied to her poems by baffled reviewers.

I once saw an absurd obstacle race on television. The competitors were tied by strong elastic cables to the starting point, and at the word *go* had to run, roll, dance, somersault or crawl as far as they could before the mean catapulting rope jerked them sharply back to the starting point. There is something of this extraordinary dance in Smith's poems, a kind of daredevil dance with poetic form. Her doggerel language, her self-mocking use of trite rhymes and ballad-like rhythms and her infectious pleasure in breaking the metrical rules as soon as she sets them up all remind me of that prancing and self-mocking race. As the elastic always jerked the competitors tumbling back, so Smith's poems jerk her unceremoniously back to the truth. They are anchored to the truth of her feelings and her own vision of the world as solidly as if that taunting jerky cable were a tentacle of her own body. The power of the work is both in its outward leap, and its tumbling back. No one knew this better than Smith herself. In performance she often sang her poems to hymn tunes in her high-pitched off-key voice. She loved to tell the story against herself of how as a child she was asked not to sing with the other girls at school because she put them off.

> My Muse sits forlorn
> She wishes she had not been born
> She sits in the cold
> No word she says is ever told.
>
> Why does my Muse only speak when she is unhappy?
> She does not, I only listen when I am unhappy
> When I am happy I live and despise writing
> For my Muse this cannot but be dispiriting.
>
> ('My Muse')

But Smith's technical sophistication is only one of the many tools she used, and the unsettling effects she achieved through juxtaposition of inappropriate ideas expressed as much the person she was as the way she worked. Her funniest poems are always sad, poignant, and searingly honest. She was never without a feeling of deep sadness, but she 'counted despair derisory' and saw it as her own weakness rather than the fault of the world. A small maker of mischief inhabited her head, a debunker of pomp and self-importance that sent her into a fit of giggling at serious moments. When she was awarded the Queen's Gold Medal for Poetry he was at work as usual:

> You feel you're with an enormously charming woman and a very professional Queen . . . She made me feel awfully like a schoolgirl again, being interviewed by a rather cordial headmistress, but knowing that headmistresses aren't always like that. Then we talked about poetry and I got rather nervous and said, 'I don't know why, but I seem to have written rather a lot about murder lately', which was rather an unfortunate thing to say . . . the smile got rather fixed.

Although she got great pleasure from receiving both this award in 1969 and the Cholmondeley Award in 1966, she could not accept such honours without a roguish twinkle. As she said of herself, 'I'm straightforward, but I'm not simple . . There is a balance; I am aware of a balance. I know the sort of things that can knock me off my balance – snakes.' And in the quiet order of her life there might well be snakes, along with the jungles and elephants.

A vigorous tug of war between her quiet suburban life in Palmers Green and the spirit-infested landscapes of her imagination generated great power in Stevie Smith's work. The source of these landscapes was Grovelands Park, at Southgate, not far from her home, and the East Coast beaches where she spent her holidays as a child. The transformation is extreme: the 'huge lake and heavenly oak trees' are dark woods and danger waters where the unearthly roam freely, malevolent or benign, spirits always vivid in the nightmare landscape.

> Over the saltings I ran. The midnight high wind
> Pulled my straight hair in streaks behind me, and I ran and ran
> And did not care, as I ran by the sea shore
> If Watchful ran behind me or waited for me
> On Northumberland Moor . . .
>
> I was running in a wood now, a wood of pine trees,
> Very dark it was and silent, I ran on brown pine needles
> Silently, and came to a gamekeeper's gallows. The mournful birds
> Hanging there cried: We are not Watchful, and an old badger
> Crawling to his sett to die said: I am not Watchful. But the wind
> Cried: Hurry! and drove great snowflakes against my face.
> Then I came to a dark house and the door swung and I went in,
> Oh Watchful, my darling, you have led me such a dance.
>                         ('Watchful, A Tale of Psyche')

The woods are always ominous, but intensely alive; the waters are always dangerous, and at the same time tempting in a disturbing way:

> He summoned up a picture of shallow sea-water
> And in it he paddled, he was a sea-walker.
>
> On an empty beach, in full sun,
> He paddled for miles and did not see anyone,
>
> And as he walked, the salty smell and the air
> Of the beautiful place, *worked*; he did not remember.
>
> That beach, as a matter of fact, shelves to deep water,
> He must be careful to remain always a coastal-walker.
>
>                         ('Night Thoughts')

In this, as in so many of Smith's poems, the danger waters are more tempting than forbidding: their temptation is most ominously celebrated in her joyful pagan poem 'The River God', and most perfectly realised in her famous and much anthologised poem 'Not Waving but Drowning'. Smith loved life, but she loved death almost more, and spent most of her life in an intricate dance with him:

> Why do I think of Death as a friend?
> It is because he is a scatterer
> He scatters the human frame
> The nerviness and the great pain . . .
>                         ('Why do I')

I love death, I think it's the most exciting thing. As one gets older one gets into this – well, it's like a race, before you get to the waterfall, when you feel the water slowly getting quicker and quicker and quicker, and you can't get out, and all you want to do is get to the waterfall and over the edge. How exciting it is!

Death is as frequent a visitor in her poems as fear and laughter, and always he is courted:

Do take Muriel out
Although your name is Death
She will not complain
When you dance her over the blasted heath.
        ('Do Take Muriel Out')

Three years after the death of her aunt Smith went to Devon to take care of her sister who had suffered a stroke. Within four months she was dead herself of a brain tumour and without much pain. Death had not failed her, 'Because death is a God, who must come when he is summoned':

Sweet Death, kind Death
Of all the gods you are the best.
        ('Why do I?')

## My Muse

My Muse is like the painting of the Court Poet and His Muse in the National Gallery; she is always howling into an indifferent ear.

It is not indifference but fear. It is the fear of a man who has a nagging wife.

It is like a coarse-grained country squire who has a fanciful wife. It is like an uneasily hearty fellow who denies his phantom. These notions of the Muse are as false as the false-hearty fellow who bites his nails because of the false picture he is making. (If he were really hearty he would not know there was anybody to listen to.)

> Why does my Muse only speak when she is unhappy?
> She does not, I only listen when I am unhappy
> When I am happy I live and despise writing
> For My Muse this cannot but be dispiriting.

This comes nearer to the truth. Here are some of the truths about poetry. She is an Angel, very strong. It is not poetry but the poet who has a feminine ending, not the Muse who is weak, but the poet. She makes a strong communication. Poetry is like a strong explosion in the sky. She makes a mushroom shape of terror and drops to the ground with a strong infection. Also she is a strong way out. The human creature is alone in his carapace. Poetry is a strong way out. The passage out that she blasts is often in splinters, covered with blood; but she can come out softly. Poetry is very light-fingered, she is like the god Hermes in my poem 'The Ambassador' (she is very light-fingered). Also she is like the horse Hermes is riding, this animal is dangerous.

> Underneath the broad hat is the face of the Ambassador
> He rides on a white horse through hell looking two ways.
> Doors open before him and shut when he has passed.
> He is master of the mysterious and in the market place
> He is known. He stole the trident, the girdle,
> The sword, the sceptre and many mechanical instruments.
> Thieves honour him. In the underworld he rides carelessly.
> Sometimes he rises into the air and flies silently.

Poetry does not like to be up to date, she refuses to be neat. ('Anglo-Saxon,' wrote Gavin Bone, 'is a good language to write poetry in because it is impossible to be neat.') All the poems Poetry writes may be called, 'Heaven, a Detail', or 'Hell, a Detail'. (She only writes about heaven and hell.) Poetry is like the goddess Thetis who turned herself into a crab with silver feet, that Peleus sought for and held.

Then in his hands she became first a fire, then a serpent, then a suffocating stench. But Peleus put sand on his hands and wrapped his body in sodden sacking and so held her through all her changes, till she became Thetis again, and so he married her, and an unhappy marriage it was. Poetry is very strong and never has any kindness at all. She is Thetis and Hermes, the Angel, the white horse and the landscape. All Poetry has to do is to make a strong communication. All the poet has to do is to listen. The poet is not an important fellow. There will always be another poet.

[1960]

# What Poems Are Made Of

Colours are what drive me most strongly, colours in painted pictures, but, most strongly of all, colours out of doors in the fresh cool air, the colours I see when I am walking in London streets, in the country or by the sea. In this northern suburb where I have lived all my life, the colours are exquisite. The streets with their bordering trees hump over red brick bridges and curve into the blue-green and white pavement perspectives where once the country lanes ran. The railway station has beige wooden canopies, lacy-edged; the advertisements are navy blue enamel with yellow lettering, the grass banks are full of flowers. When we first came here it was a country place and we still have the great parks that were once private estates, with their great oak trees and grasslands. There is also a great deep lake which in hard winters is frozen so that you can walk on it.

> Underneath the frozen water
> Steps the Lord of Ullan's daughter
> She is a witch of endless might
> And treads the borders of the night.

I like to walk across Hyde Park where the loving couples lie:

> I fear the ladies and gentlemen under the trees,
> Could any of them make an affectionate partner and not tease? –
> Oh, the affectionate sensitive mind is not easy to please.

And then cross into Wilton Place and see the pale grey Italianate houses that stand so delicate in their crescent curve they seem, like St David's Cathedral in Pembrokeshire, to be made of Indian paper.

There is much to be seen in city streets that stirs the heart:

> Sisley
> Walked so nicely
> With footsteps so discreet
> To see her pass
> You'd never guess
> She walked upon the street.

> Down where the Liffey waters' turgid flood
> Churns up to greet the ocean-driven mud,
> A bruiser in a fix
> Murdered her for 6/6.

But I like sea and country best – and the parks. I like to watch people in our park. What are they talking about? Perhaps this:

> He told his life story to Mrs Courtly
> Who was a widow. 'Let us get married shortly',
> He said. 'I am no longer passionate,
> But we can have some conversation before it is too late.'

Our park is a happy place even when it is raining.

I also like to watch the birds, animals and children, and to think how fortunate I am they are not mine. I do not know how people can manage to have animals, wives and children and also write. Of course isolation can be very painful. Many of my poems are about the pains of isolation, but once the poem is written, the happiness of being alone comes flooding back. In this next poem the lonely person was so foolish as not to recognise his nature and its solace. He should have remembered the schoolroom tag: *Fata nolentuem trahunt, volentem ducunt* (the fates drag the unwilling, the willing they lead). Instead he tried to do some war work:

> To those who are isolate
> War comes, promising respite,
> Making what seems to be up to the moment
>     the most successful endeavour
> Against the fort of the failed spirit
>     that is alone for ever.
> Spurious failed spirit, adamantine wasture,
> Crop, spirit, crop thy stony pasture!

It is not a stony pasture.

Why are so many of my poems about death, if I am having such an enjoyable time all the time? Partly because I am haunted by the fear of what might have happened if I had not been able to draw back in time from the husband-wives-children and pet animals situation in which I surely should have failed.

I admire very much the people who make a success of this difficult situation, that can be also so rich and splendid, for love and comfort. I see a mother and her child, standing by a greengrocer's stall; they are poor people, poorly clad:

> Mother, I love you so.
> Said the child, I love you more than you know.
> She laid her head on her mother's arm,
> And the love between them kept them warm.

But sometimes love is demanded. That does not go so well. I imagine this: that a little child has been turned to stone in his mother's lap. She clutches him and cries:

> I'll have your heart, if not by gift my knife
> Shall carve it out. I'll have your heart, your life.

Not all my poems come to me from what I watch and see and from the colours I love. Many come from books I read (I almost never read poetry), especially from the books I am sent for reviewing, which are often books on controversial subjects, such as history and theology. From the printed page, a counter-argument will strike up in my mind. From this poems often come. There is pleasure in this, but pain, too, because of the pressure on the nerves; for all human beings it is like this. I love Death because he breaks the human pattern and frees us from pleasures too prolonged as well as from the pains of this world. It is pleasant, too, to remember that Death lies in our hands; he must come if we call him. 'Dost thou see the precipice?' Seneca said to the poor oppressed slave (meaning he could always go and jump off it). I think if there were no death, life would be more than flesh and blood could bear:

> My heart goes out to my Creator in love
> Who gave me Death, as end and remedy.
> All living creatures come to quiet Death
> For him to eat up their activity
> And give them nothing, which is what they want although
> When they are living they do not think so.

[1969]

STEVIE SMITH

## The Frog Prince

I am a frog
I live under a spell
I live at the bottom
Of a green well

And here I must wait
Until a maiden places me
On her royal pillow
And kisses me
In her father's palace.

The story is familiar
Everybody knows it well
But do other enchanted people feel as nervous
As I do? The stories do not tell,

Ask if they will be happier
When the changes come
As already they are fairly happy
In a frog's doom?

I have been a frog now
For a hundred years
And in all this time
I have not shed many tears,

I am happy, I like the life,
Can swim for many a mile
(When I have hopped to the river)
And am for ever agile.

And the quietness,
Yes, I like to be quiet
I am habituated
To a quiet life,

But always when I think these thoughts
As I sit in my well
Another thought comes to me and says:
It is part of the spell

To be happy
To work up contentment
To make much of being a frog
To fear disenchantment

Says, It will be *heavenly*
To be set free,
Cries, *Heavenly* the girl who disenchants
And the royal times, *heavenly*,
And I think it will be.

Come then, royal girl and royal times,
Come quickly,
I can be happy until you come
But I cannot be heavenly,
Only disenchanted people
Can be heavenly.


**I rode with my darling . . .**


I rode with my darling in the dark wood at night
And suddenly there was an angel burning bright
Come with me or go far away he said
But do not stay alone in the dark wood at night.

My darling grew pale he was responsible
He said we should go back it was reasonable
But I wished to stay with the angel in the dark wood at night.

My darling said goodbye and rode off angrily
And suddenly I rode after him and came to a cornfield
Where had my darling gone and where was the angel now?
The wind bent the corn and drew it along the ground
And the corn said, Do not go alone in the dark wood.

Then the wind drew more strongly and black clouds covered the moon
And I rode into the dark wood at night.

There was a light burning in the trees but it was not the angel
And in the pale light stood a tall tower without windows
And a mean rain fell and the voice of the tower spoke,

Do not stay alone in the dark wood at night.

The walls of the pale tower were heavy, in a heavy mood
The great stones stood as if resisting without belief.
Oh how sad sighed the wind, how disconsolately,
Do not ride alone in the dark wood at night.

Loved I once my darling? I love him not now.
Had I a mother beloved? She lies far away.
A sister, a loving heart? My aunt a noble lady?
All all is silent in the dark wood at night.


## / Touch and Go

Man is coming out of the mountains
But his tail is caught in the pass.
Why does he not free himself
Is he not an ass?

Do not be impatient with him
He is bowed with passion and fret
He is not out of the mountains
He is not half out yet.

Look at his sorrowful eyes
His torn cheeks, his brow
He lies with his head in the dust
Is there no one to help him now?

No, there is no one to help him
Let him get on with it
Cry the ancient enemies of man
As they cough and spit.

The enemies of man are like trees
They stand with the sun in their branches
Is there no one to help my creature
Where he languishes?

Ah, the delicate creature
He lies with his head in the rubble

Pray that the moment pass
And the trouble.

Look he moves, that is more than a prayer,
But he is so slow
Will he come out of the mountains?
It is touch and go.


## Major Macroo

Major Hawkaby Cole Macroo
Chose
Very wisely
A patient Griselda of a wife with a heart of gold
That never beat for a soul but him
Himself and his slightest whim.

He left her alone for months at a time
When he had to have a change
Just had to
And his pension wouldn't stretch to a fare for two
And he didn't want it to.

And if she wept she was game and nobody knew it
And she stood at the edge of the tunnel and waved as his train went
          through it.

And because it was cheaper they lived abroad
And did he care if she might be unhappy or bored?
He did not.
He'd other things to think of – a lot.

He'd fads and he fed them fat,
And she could lump it and that was that.

He'd several boy friends
And she thought it was nice for him to have them,
And she loved him and felt that he needed her and waited
And waited and never became exasperated.

Even his room
Was dusted and kept the same,

And when friends came
They went into every room in the house but that one
Which Hawkaby wouldn't have shown.

Such men as these, such selfish cruel men
Hurting what most they love what most loves them,
Never make a mistake when it comes to choosing a woman
To cherish them and be neglected and not think it inhuman.

## Man is a Spirit

Man is a spirit. This the poor flesh knows,
Yet serves him well for host when the wind blows,
Why should this guest go wrinkling up his nose?

## The Small Lady

In front of the mighty washing machine
The small lady stood in a beautiful dream,
'That these clothes so clean (oh what a relief)
    Must still be ironed, is my only grief.'

But then came a great witch passing on the air
Who said, 'What is it you still wish for, my pretty dear?
Would you like to be a duck on a northern lake,
A milky white duck with a yellow beak?'
'Aroint thee, false witch!' cried the lady with a brave face,
'Human inventions help properly, magic is a disgrace.'
The witch flew off cackling for the harm was done,
'I smell water,' cried the lady and followed her into the setting sun.
And now in a false shape, on the wind-driven black pelt
Of that far northern lake, she is without help:
Crying, Away, away,
Come, ray of the setting sun,
Over the lake
Spread thy red streak,
Light my kingdom.

Heart of my heart, it is a mournful song,
Never will this poor lady come home.

## The River God

I may be smelly and I may be old,
Rough in my pebbles, reedy in my pools,
But where my fish float by I bless their swimming
And I like the people to bathe in me, especially women.
But I can drown the fools
Who bathe too close to the weir, contrary to rules.
And they take a long time drowning
As I throw them up now and then in a spirit of clowning.
Hi yih, yippity-yap, merrily I flow,
O I may be an old foul river but I have plenty of go.
Once there was a lady who was too bold
She bathed in me by the tall black cliff where the water runs cold,
So I brought her down here
To be my beautiful dear.
Oh will she stay with me will she stay
This beautiful lady, or will she go away?
She lies in my beautiful deep river bed with many a weed
To hold her, and many a waving reed.
Oh who would guess what a beautiful white face lies there
Waiting for me to smooth and wash away the fear
She looks at me with. Hi yih, do not let her
Go. There is no one on earth who does not forget her
Now. They say I am a foolish old smelly river
But they do not know of my wide original bed
Where the lady waits, with her golden sleepy head.
If she wishes to go I will not forgive her.

## Brickenden, Hertfordshire

Sitting alone of a summer's evening,
I thought
Of the tragedy of unwatered country.
O little village of Brickenden,
Where is thy stream,
Translucent drain of thy manorial sward?
Thy sward is green,
Its source of verdancy guessed but unseen.
Where is thy stream?

I have beat every bound of this wild wood.
I have trod down its spiteful and detaining undergrowth,
Seeking a broad stream and contented fish,
Seeking but finding not.
Now that the sun
Sou'westering in the sky
Tells me that evening is come,
I rest
Oppressed
By thy wood's profligate viridity,
By thy wood's sap,
Child of a moisture that I cannot tap.

O woods of Brickenden, you have confounded me
By your appearance of humidity.
I see the pashy ground,
And round and round
My tired feet the rushes twine,
And frogs croak and the sweating slime
Is moved about by an ambiguous brood
Of low and legless life.
Hadst thou thy stream,
O wood of Brickenden,
This had been
Paradise.

But thy sap's virtue comes from dank earth's sweat,
And to be wet
Is not enough, O wood.
Hadst thou thy stream,
O little village of Brickenden,
Thy stream
Had salined thee
By virtue of destinatory sea,
And thou hadst been
A Paradise.
But lacking stream
Art but a suppuration of earth's humours.
Sitting alone on a summer's evening,
I wept
For the tragedy of unwatered country.
Take thou my tears, O Brickenden,
They are thy rank sweat's sea.

## To Carry the Child

To carry the child into adult life
Is good? I say it is not,
To carry the child into adult life
Is to be handicapped.

The child in adult life is defenceless
And if he is grown-up, knows it,
And the grown-up looks at the childish part
And despises it.

The child, too, despises the clever grown-up,
The man-of-the-world, the frozen,
For the child has the tears alive on his cheek
And the man has none of them.

As the child has colours, and the man sees no
Colours or anything,
Being easy only in things of the mind,
The child is easy in feeling.

Easy in feeling, easily excessive
And in excess powerful,
For instance, if you do not speak to the child
He will make trouble.

You would say a man had the upper hand
Of the child, if a child survive,
I say the child has fingers of strength
To strangle the man alive.

Oh it is not happy, it is never happy,
To carry the child into adulthood,
Let children lie down before full growth
And die in their infanthood

And be guilty of no man's blood.

But oh the poor child, the poor child, what can he do,
Trapped in a grown-up carapace,
But peer outside of his prison room
With the eye of an anarchist?

## In the Park

Walking one day in the park in winter
I heard two silvered gentlemen talking,
Two old friends, elderly, walking, talking
There by the silver lake mid-pooled black in winter.

'Pray for the Mute who have no word to say,'
Cried the one old gentleman, 'Not because they are dumb,
But they are weak. And the weak thoughts beating in the brain
Generate a sort of heat, yet cannot speak.
Thoughts that are bound without sound
In the tomb of the brain's room, wound. Pray for the Mute.'

'But' (said his friend), 'see how they swim
Free in the element best loved, so wet; yet breathe
As a visitor to the air come; plunge then, rejoicing more,
Having left it briefly for the visited shore, to come
Home to the wet
Windings that are yet
Best loved though familiar; and oh so right the wet
Stream and the wave; he is their pet.'

Finished, the mild friend
Smiled, put aside his well-tuned hearing instrument
And it seemed
The happiness he spoke of
Irradiated all his members, and his heart
Barked with delight to stress
So much another's happiness.

But which other's? The sombre first
Speaker reversed
The happy moment; cried again
(Mousing for pain) 'Pray for the Mute' (a tear drops)
'They are like the brute.'

Struck by the shout
That he may not know what it's about
The deaf friend again
Up-ends his hearing instrument to relieve the strain.
What? Oh shock, ' "Pray for the Mute"?
I thought you said the newt.'

Now which is Christianer pray, of these old friends, the one who will
      say
For pain's sake pray, pray; or the deaf other that rejoices
So much that the cool amphibian
Shall have his happiness, all things rejoicing with him?

But wait; the first speaker now, the old sombre one,
Is penetrated quite by his friend's sun
And, 'Oh blessed you,' he cries, 'to show
So in simplicity what is true.'
All his face is suffused with happy tears and as he weeps he sings a
      happy song,
Happier even than his friend's song was, righting the wrong.
So two, better than one, finally strike truth in this happy song:

'Praise,' cries the weeping softened one, 'Not pray, praise, all men,
Praise is the best prayer, the least self's there, that least's release.'


## Scorpion

'This night shall thy soul be required of thee'
*My* soul is never required of *me*
It always has to be somebody else of course
Will my soul be required of me tonight perhaps?

(I often wonder what it will be like
To have one's soul required of one
But all I can think of is the Out-Patients' Department –
'Are you Mrs Briggs, dear?'
No, I am Scorpion.)

I should like my soul to be required of me, so as
To waft over grass till it comes to the blue sea
I am very fond of grass, I always have been, but there must
Be no cow, person or house to be seen.

Sea and *grass* must be quite empty
Other souls can find somewhere *else*.

O Lord God please come
And require the soul of thy Scorpion

Scorpion so wishes to be gone.

# KATHLEEN RAINE

**Kathleen Raine** was born in 1908, and grew up in London and Northumberland. She studied natural sciences at Cambridge. As well as thirteen books of poems, she has published works of criticism, and has an international reputation as a scholar of Blake, Yeats, and other aspects of the Neoplatonic tradition in English Romantic poetry.

Her home is in London, where she has recently established the magazine *Temenos*, a review dedicated to the arts of the imagination. Three collections of poetry, her autobiography and a number of critical and scholarly works have been translated into French, and several other books have appeared in Italian, Norwegian, Spanish and Japanese.

Kathleen Raine first published a *Collected Poems* in 1956, and in 1981 the present *Collected Poems 1935-1980* appeared from Allen and Unwin. Her recent books of poems include *The Lost Country* (1971), *On a Deserted Shore* (1973), *The Oval Portrait* (1977), and *The Oracle in the Heart* (1980). Eighteen of her books are currently available, including *The Inner Journey of the Poet* (1982) and *World Within a World* (1982). Her three-volume autobiography, published by Hamish Hamilton, comprises *Farewell Happy Fields* (1973), *The Land Unknown* (1975) and *The Lion's Mouth* (1977).

The roots of my poetry go back for more generations than I can trace them. I have written of my childhood in the first volume of my autobiography, *Farewell Happy Fields* – of the rich world of a country childhood in Northumberland during the First World War, and of the very different inheritances I received from each of my parents. On my mother's side I inherited Scotland's songs and ballads – lowland Scotland, not the Gaelic Highlands, which has another culture altogether – sung or recited by my mother, aunts and grandmothers, who had learned them from *their* mothers and grandmothers before universal literacy destroyed an oral tradition and culture that scarcely any longer exists. The number of songs and ballads my mother and my aunts knew seemed endless, for memory, uncluttered by the daily chatter of radio and television, retained whole unwritten volumes of songs and stories. My mother's memory for poetry was remarkable, and besides her Scottish songs and ballads she could, even in her old age, repeat long passages from Milton and many other English poets whom she loved. The Bible was daily reading in my childhood, and I learned, both at home and at school, many psalms and passages from the New Testament by heart, words perhaps barely understood at the time, to be recalled in later years when their full meaning could bring consolation or wisdom in time of need. It is the words we have by heart that are ours, are part of us in a way that words we merely read, enjoy and forget, never can be. I am glad that I grew up in a world in which the memorising of the great literature – Shakespeare and the Bible especially – was an essential part of education.

My father was the English master at the County High School, Ilford. His native county however was Durham, and for Durham University he had written his M.Litt. thesis on Wordsworth, a fellow north-countryman; but his real love was Shakespeare, and he never missed an opportunity of taking me and my mother to see Shakespeare acted. I first saw Hamlet played by a repertory company not at Stratford-on-Avon but at Stratford-atte-Bow. From my father I learned to love the English language and its Latin and Old English roots, to see words as the embodiment of centuries of human thought and experience. From my father also I learned to regard the words of the great poets as expressions of the same order of truth (though in a lesser degree) as we found in the Bible. Both were "inspired" from beyond the everyday human mind, and were expressions of a knowledge different in kind from the natural knowledge we gather from everyday experience or scientific experiment. This "inspired" character was indeed the mark of what we called poetry; not something invented but something given; something that gave a kind of luminosity to even some quite slight poems by minor poets. There was of course also comic verse and satire, which were clever and ingenious, but not, in the true sense, "poetry", which was rather a quality of experience – 'the poetry of life' as my father would have said – than a form of words. It was not the purpose of poetry to record anything and everything, to merely describe either the outer world or some subjective mood, but to speak from the imagination of the poet to the imagination of the reader.

Brought up as I was in a household in which the poets were so regarded it naturally became my ambition to become a poet. I confided this intention one day to my father as we bicycled to the school where he taught and I studied, and was much surprised at the cool and sceptical reception he gave to this proposal which I had thought would have pleased him, as a clergyman or a doctor might have been pleased to know that a son wished to follow his father's profession. But to my father the poets belonged to a higher world, to another plane; to say one wished to become a poet was to him something like saying one proposed to write a fifth Gospel.

But for my mother the world of poetry was close at hand; it was the world in which she herself actually lived her life. It was she who wrote down my baby-poems in a book before I could hold a pencil and write my own; and then she kept those as well. In retrospect it seems to me that she implanted in me the habit of making poems in imitation of those she sung or said to me. I have often thought that it is *her* desire I have fulfilled, for to her poetry was the very essence of life. I used then to think that everyone must want to be a poet, and that only by sacrificing that one desire, which all must have, did some become milkmen, or businessmen or follow some other joyless trade. And if Blake is right in declaring that every man and woman should practise one of the arts of Imagination – painting, music, poetry and architecture – perhaps I was right; by what straying away from our true identity do we become enslaved to the meaningless tasks created by a soulless technocracy?

Beyond that early formation I am grateful for an excellent education, for acquiring the discipline of work and a respect for exact knowledge. I left school with an Exhibition in Natural Sciences from Girton College, Cambridge, where I studied botany and zoology. Why not English literature? Because, for me, literature and poetry had nothing to do with "school", they were part of life: why study as an academic subject the literature of one's own language, which one reads as a matter of course? I have since read most of English literature, much French, and in translation half the wisdom of the world. Reading, like travel, leads one on and on, yet it is impossible to have visited all the 'realms of gold' just as it is impossible to visit more than a few of the innumerable places of this beautiful earth. Both kinds of exploration are endlessly enriching. But at a certain point each of us has to discover what is our own and which among the gifts offered to us, tangible and intangible, we need and can make use of.

I have gone on all my life reading and studying and am, I suppose, comparatively learned, at least in my chosen field of study (William Blake and his sources and the Neoplatonic tradition in English literature). All this has enriched my own poetry, and, ultimately, simplified it too; for whereas, when I was young, I was impressed by complexity and a display of learning in verse (I think of the kind of poetry my Cambridge contemporary and friend William Empson was writing), I have come to understand that the profound themes can – and must – be expressed with great simplicity. Not that all simple verse is profound, or all verbally rich and complex verse superficial (I think of Dylan Thomas, Vernon Watkins and David Jones) but my own method has increasingly been to pack much meaning into few words. I hope to stir vibrations on several levels; and when a reader asks in certain of my poems 'does the world (or the sentence) mean this, that?' the answer is very often that both meanings (perhaps many meanings) are meant to vibrate together, like a chord of music. I therefore use much care in the arrangement of simple words.

Blake wrote 'Improvement makes strait roads; but the crooked roads without Improvement are roads of genius.' Improvement comes from without; genius summons from within. My teachers used to impress upon us that genius is an 'infinite capacity for taking pains'. True genius may demand that we do take infinite pains, but that is not in itself "genius". Rather it is "inspiration", the summoning from within of an "other" mind, beyond our trivial daily mind. And it is not poets and musicians only who know this 'crisis that unites for certain moments the sleeping and the waking mind' – so Yeats defines it – but mathematicians, physicists, imaginative thinkers of every kind. This "other" mind poets once called the Muse; modern psychology has other and longer names for it; Yeats called it the 'age-old memoried self' whose memories go back far beyond ours and belong to 'the soul of the world'. That is why poets do not follow the beaten tracks; they serve another master.

Not that poets are by any means all rebels, drop-outs, ignor-amuses, revolutionaries, or drinkers in pubs; merely that Imagin-ation knows the way it must take and creates for each of us the appropriate situation. I have known poets of all stations of life. T.S.

Eliot was a successful banker and then a publisher; Herbert Read a curator at the Victoria and Albert Museum; Yeats a theatre-manager and later a senator; Vernon Watkins escaped not from, but *to* a bank in Swansea. Comparing myself with these I feel some shame that, well qualified as I was to engage in many of the hard and useful tasks of the world, I could never persuade my *daimon* to let me settle down to a quiet and useful practical life, as in certain moods I think that perhaps I should have done or perhaps what I ought rather to regret is the meagreness of my contribution to poetry.

By the standards of the outer world it might seem that poetry comes from some invisible grain of sand in the sensitive organism, or a wound compensated by the growth of the pearl or ambergris of poetry. Yeats wrote that 'The intellect of man is forced to choose/ Perfection of the life or of the work.' Like everyone else I would have liked to have my cake and eat it, but that hard choice has again and again been forced upon me – or rather I have again and again been forced back to it much against my will – every gain of the poet being counterbalanced by some corresponding sacrifice of life. Or perhaps there never was any choice, and I took the only way I could ever have taken. The price, for myself and for others has been high – too high, perhaps, for a handful of verses.

But the poet is not allowed to serve two masters. We serve an inner living universe of far greater authority than the voices which tell us what we ought and ought not to be doing from a practical point of view. I have always found, in fact, that when we follow that inner guidance somehow or other practical solutions are always forthcoming; we live by miracle. My Inspirer has always been very real to me; not the feminine figure of the muse, but as it were the *puer eternus*, the Eternal Child, an unageing presence nearer and more intimate than friend or lover, and not to be denied, at the price of life itself – imaginative life that is, a life that, once tasted, the poet cannot endure to be parted from. A Greek legend tells how Bellerophon, who once rode Pegasus, the winged horse of inspiration, through some folly or betrayal was thrown to the ground and went limping through life thereafter.

There is something of the poet in all of us, of course, or of the painter or the musician or the dancer or the architect. But of all the arts the living of a life is perhaps the greatest; to live every moment of life with the same imaginative commitment as the poet brings to a special field. The fashion in a society whose values are material and which sets little store on any other asks not what we "are" but what we "do"; worse, the phrase "what is he worth?" has come to mean, "How much money has he?" How sad, how false, and what a betrayal! What we are "worth" is not what we have, not even what we have made or done, but what we are. Poetry is not an end in itself but in the service of life; of what use are poems, or any other works of art, unless to enable human lives to be lived with insight of a deeper kind, with more sensitive feelings, more intense sense of the beautiful, with deeper understanding? According to Plato the soul knows everything, but in this world has forgotten; and the poem reminds us of what we ourselves know, but did not know we knew; reminds us, above all, of what we are.

KATHLEEN RAINE

## Amo Ergo Sum

Because I love
    The sun pours out its rays of living gold
    Pours out its gold and silver on the sea.

Because I love
    The earth upon her astral spindle winds
    Her ecstasy-producing dance.

Because I love
    Clouds travel on the winds through wide skies,
    Skies wide and beautiful, blue and deep.

Because I love
    Wind blows white sails,
    The wind blows over flowers, the sweet wind blows.

Because I love
    The ferns grow green, and green the grass, and green
    The transparent sunlit trees.

Because I love
    Larks rise up from the grass
    And all the leaves are full of singing birds.

Because I love
    The summer air quivers with a thousand wings,
    Myriads of jewelled eyes burn in the light.

Because I love
    The iridescent shells upon the sand
    Take forms as fine and intricate as thought.

Because I love
    There is an invisible way across the sky,
    Birds travel by that way, the sun and moon
    And all the stars travel that path by night.

Because I love
    There is a river flowing all night long.

Because I love
    All night the river flows into my sleep,
    Ten thousand living things are sleeping in my arms,
    And sleeping wake, and flowing are at rest.

## Heirloom

She gave me childhood's flowers,
Heather and wild thyme,
Eyebright and tormentil,
Lichen's mealy cup
Dry on wind-scored stone,
The corbies on the rock,
The rowan by the burn.

Sea-marvels a child beheld
Out in the fisherman's boat,
Fringed pulsing violet
Medusa, sea-gooseberries,
Starfish on the sea-floor,
Cowries and rainbow-shells
From pools on a rocky shore.

Gave me her memories,
But kept her last treasure:
'When I was a lass', she said,
'Sitting among the heather,
'Suddenly I saw
'That all the moor was alive!
'I have told no-one before'.

That was my mother's tale.
Seventy years had gone
Since she saw the living skein
Of which the world is woven,
And having seen, knew all;
Through long indifferent years
Treasuring the priceless pearl.

*From* **On a Deserted Shore**


Great the domain of love:
Farther than eye can see
From my small house of life
Realms of your new state encompass me.

                    *

Sun gives no light
And days like shadows pass.
Shut by the lids of sense, my blinded gaze
Cannot discern your spirit bright.

                    *

Cadence of an old song from Eriskay
Tells the heart's story:
From dissonance of the world I turn away
Not to evade but to descry
Lineaments of humanity.

                    *

Grief's metamorphoses:
Anguish, small pregnant seed,
Becomes a worm that gnaws through years,
At last quiescent lies; not dead;
Till waking, what winged impulse takes the skies?

                    *

'Made to be broken,' a lover said
Who knew the heart
That breaks and breaks again,
And yet will not believe
That love is born to grief.

                    *

Not sorrow breaks the heart
But an imagined joy
So dear it cannot be
But we have elsewhere known
The lost estate we mourn.

Whole that has made me,
Whose stress and weight
Creates and will destroy,
Each part, I find,
Bears always all the world.

*

Downcast on the ground,
The form of spirit
We are but do not know
Save by a shadow
Distorted, earthbound.

*

You who cast no shadow, nowhere, everywhere,
All that you loved you are,
Sun's gold on the sea, waves far out from the shore,
Flowing for ever.

*

Blue serene wide sky
Where sight runs free, joy
Of unbounded light:
It is as if we meet.

*

Dream, shadow of hope and fear,
Secret foreshadower, guide
Of all souls, living and dead,
What the unwinding and inwinding thread
But heart's desire?

*

I am content to be
At last what first we were,
Grass of the one hill,
Water of one pool,
Breath of the same air,
Sight of the single eye.

C

## 'I felt, under my old breasts, this April day'

I felt, under my old breasts, this April day,
Young breasts, like leaf and flower to come, under gray apple-buds
And heard a young girl within me say,
'Let me be free of this winter bark, this toil-worn body,
'I who am young,
'My form subtle as a dream'.
And I replied, 'You, who are I,
'Entered a sad house when you put on my clay.
'This shabby menial self, and life-long time,
'Bear with as you may
'Until your ripening joy
'Put off the dust and ashes that I am,
'Like winter scales cast from the living tree.'


## The Dead

Not because they are far, but because so near
The dead seem strange to us;
Stripped of those unprized familiar forms they wore,
Defending from our power to wound
That poignant naked thing they were,
The holy souls
Speak, essence to essence, heart to heart.
Scarcely can we dare
To know in such intimacy
Those whom courtesy, or reticence, or fear
Hid, when, covered in skins of beasts,
Evading and evaded,
We turned the faces of our souls away.
Only the youngest child is as near as they,
Or those who share the marriage-bed
When pity and tenderness dwell there.

## Self

Who am I, who
Speaks from the dust,
Who looks from the clay?

Who hears
For the mute stone,
For fragile water feels
With finger and bone?

Who for the forest breathes the evening,
Sees for the rose,
Who knows
What the bird sings?

Who am I, who for the sun fears
The demon dark,
In order holds
Atom and chaos?

Who out of nothingness has gazed
On the beloved face?


## The Mirage

No, I have seen the mirage tremble, seen how thin
The veil stretched over apparent time and space
To make the habitable earth, the enclosed garden.

I saw on a bare hillside an ash-tree stand
And all its intricate branches suddenly
Failed, as I gazed, to be a tree,
And road and hillside failed to make a world.
Hill, tree, sky, distance, only seemed to be
And I saw nothing I could give a name,
Not any name known to the heart.

What failed? The retina received
The differing waves of light, or rays of darkness,
Eyes, hands, all senses brought me
Messages that lifelong I had believed.
Appearances that once composed reality
Here turned to dust, to mist, to motes in the eye
Or like the reflection broken on a pool
The unrelated visual fragment foundered
On a commotion of those deeps
Where earth floats safe, when waves are still.

The living instrument
When fingers gently touch the strings,
Or when a quiet wind
Blows through the reed, makes music of birds,
Song, words, the human voice.
Too strong a blast,
A blow too heavy breaks and silences
The singer and the song;
A grief too violent
Wrecks the image of the world, on waves whose amplitude
Beats beyond the compass of the heart.

The waves subside, the image reassembles:
There was a tree once more, hills, and the world,
But I have seen the emptiness of air
Ready to swallow up the bird in its flight,
Or note of music, or winged word, the void
That traps the rabbit on cropped turf as in a snare,
Lies at the heart of the wren's warm living eggs,
In pollen dust of summer flowers, opens
Within the smallest seed of grass, the abyss
That now and always underlies the hills.


**Night Sky**


There came such clear opening of the night sky,
The deep glass of wonders, the dark mind
In unclouded gaze of the abyss
Opened like the expression of a face.

I looked into that clarity where all things are
End and beginning, and saw
My destiny there: 'So', I said, 'no other
'Was possible ever. This
'Is I. The pattern stands so for ever.'

What am I? Bound and bounded,
A pattern among the stars, a point in motion
Tracing my way. I am my way: it is I
I travel among the wonders.
Held in that gaze and known
In the eye of the abyss,
'Let it be so', I said,
And my heart laughed with joy
To know the death I must die.


## Scala Coeli


We do not see them come,
Their great wings furled, their boundless forms infolded
Smaller than poppy-seed or grain of corn
To enter the dimensions of our world,
In time to unfold what in eternity they are,
Each a great sun, but dwindled to a star
By the distances they have travelled.

Higher than cupola their bright ingress;
Presences vaster than the vault of night,
Incorporeal mental spaces infinite
Diminished to a point and to a moment brought
Through the everywhere and nowhere invisible door
By the many ways they know
The thoughts of wisdom pass.
In seed that drifts in air, or on the water's flow
They come to us down ages long as dreams
Or instantaneous as delight.

As from seed, tree flower and fruit
Grow and fade like a dissolving cloud,
Or as the impress of the wind

Makes waves and ripples spread,
They move unseen across our times and spaces.
We try to hold them, trace on walls
Of cave, cave-temple or monastic cell their shadows cast:
Animal-forms, warriors, dancers, winged angels, words of power
On precious leaves inscribed in gold or lapis lazuli,
Or arabesques in likeness of the ever-flowing.

They show us gardens of Paradise, holy mountains
Where water of life springs from rock or lion's mouth;
Walk with us unseen, put into our hands emblems,
An ear of corn, pine-cone, lotus, looking-glass or chalice;
As dolphin, peacock, hare or moth or serpent show themselves,
Or human-formed, a veiled bride, a boy bearing a torch,
Shrouded or robed or crowned, four-faced,
Sounding lyre or sistrum, or crying in bird-voices;
Water and dust and light
Reflect their images as they slowly come and swiftly pass.

We do not see them go
From visible into invisible like gossamer in the sun.
Bodies by spirit raised
Fall as dust to dust when the wind drops
Moth-wing and chrysalis.
Those who live us and outlive us do not stay,
But leave empty their semblances, icons, bodies
Of long-enduring gold, or the fleet golden flower
On which the Buddha smiled.
In vain we look for them where others found them,
For by the vanishing stair of time immortals are for ever departing;
But while we gaze after the receding vision
Others are already descending through gates of ivory and horn.

### 'Long ago I thought you young, bright daimon'

Long ago I though you young, bright daimon,
Whisperer in my ear
Of springs of water, leaves and song of birds,
By all time younger
Than I, who from the day of my conception

Began to age into experience and pain;
But now life in its cycle swings out of time again
I see how old you were,
Older by eternity than I, who, my hair gray,
Eyes dim with reading books,
Can never fathom those grave deep memories
Whose messenger you are,
Day-spring to the young, and to the old, ancient of days.


## Turner's Seas

We call them beautiful,
Turner's appalling seas, shipwreck and deluge
Where man's contraptions, mast and hull,
Lurch, capsize, shatter to driftwood in the whelming surge and swell,
Men and women like spindrift hurled in spray
And no survivors in those sliding glassy graves.
Doomed seafarers on unfathomed waters,
We yet call beautiful those gleaming gulphs that break in foam,
Beautiful the storm-foreboding skies, the lurid west,
Beautiful the white radiance that dissolves all.
What recognition from what deep source cries
Glory to the universal light that walks the ever-running waves,
What memory deeper than fear, what recollection of untrammelled
            joy
Our scattered falling drops retain of gleaming ocean's unending
            play?


## 'Behind the lids of sleep'

Behind the lids of sleep
In what clear river
Do the maimed, the misshapen
Bathe slender feet?
From what sky, what mountain
Do these waters pour
That wash away the stain
Of the world's mire?

On what journey
Does the night-traveller go
In quest of what lost treasure?
In what holy land
The mysteries shown,
Meaning beyond words and measure,
In what cave what ear of wheat?

Behind closed lids
The toil-worn stray
In fields not sown.
In childless arms a child is laid,
And, stilled with awe,
A bodiless mourner hears
A harmony too deep for senses dulled with pain.

By secret ways
The old revisit some long-vanished house
Once home, open a door
Where the long dead, made young again,
Offer the food of dream
That none may taste who would return.

Each to our own place
We go where none may follow
Nor hurt nor harm
The gentle wanderer whose waking days
Are exile, and whose slumbering form,
Vesture of soul clay cannot soil
Nor years deface,
Shabby and travel-worn.

# DENISE LEVERTOV

**Denise Levertov** was born in 1923 and grew up in Ilford, Essex. She was educated at home by her father, a Russian Jewish immigrant who became an Anglican priest, and by her Welsh mother. Her first book of poems, *The Double Image*, was published by the Cresset Press, London, in 1946. Two more collections were published in Britain by Cape, in 1965 and 1968.

In 1948 she moved to America, and was published in Kenneth Rexroth's anthology *The New British Poets*. 'She, more than anyone else,' Rexroth was to write later, 'had led the redirection of American poetry . . . to the mainstream of world literature.'

All of Levertov's books are published by New Directions in America. Her first six collections are combined in *Collected Earlier Poems 1940-1960* and in *Poems 1960-1967*. Also available are the collections *Relearning the Alphabet* (1970), *To Stay Alive* (1971), *Footprints* (1972), *The Freeing of the Dust* (1975), *Life in the Forest* (1978) and *Candles in Babylon* (1982), translations of the French poet Guillevic (1969), and two prose collections, *The Poet in the World* (1973) and *Light Up the Cave* (1981). In 1985 her *Selected Poems* and a new collection, *Oblique Prayers*, will be published in Britain by Bloodaxe.

'Who are you? and how did you become what you are?' are questions which, when I try to answer them honestly, increase my awareness of how strong, in my case (where in others place and community often play a dominant part) were inherited tendencies and the influence of the cultural milieu – unsupported by a community – of my own family. My father's Hasidic ancestry, his being steeped in Jewish and Christian scholarship and mysticism, his fervor and eloquence as a preacher, were factors built into my cells even though I rarely paid conscious heed to what, as a child, I mostly felt were parts of the embarrassing adult world, and which during my adolescence I rejected as restrictive. Similarly, my mother's Welsh intensity and lyric feeling for Nature were not just the air I breathed but, surely, were in the body I breathed with. Reading, at 60, the out-of-print or manuscript pages of my father's theological writings, or the poems my mother took (shyly) to writing in her late 70s and 80s, I see clearly how much they, though not dedicated to the vocation of poetry, were nevertheless protopoets.

When I say the cultural atmosphere of our household was unsupported by a community I refer to the fact that my parents – he a converted Russian Jew who, after spending the First World War teaching at the University of Leipzig (though under semi-house arrest as an "enemy alien"), settled in England and was ordained as a priest of the Anglican Church; she a Welshwoman who had grown up in a mining village and later in a North Wales country town, and subsequently travelled widely – were exotic birds in the plain English coppice of Ilford, Essex. Even though our house was semi-detached and exactly like its neighbors architecturally, it looked different because it had no half-curtains or venetian blinds like the others, only side-curtains on its large windows, so passers-by could look right in; and what they could see included bookshelves in every room, while in the bay window of my father's upstairs study was an almost lifesize stone statue representing Jesus preaching, which caused strangers to stare and cross the street to get a better look at it. And my mother's front garden, though more restrained than the larger back garden, was never prim like many of the others along the street but suggested a foreign opulence, especially when the California poppies – later to delight homesick G.I.s billeted down the road – were in full orange glory.

The Levertoffs lived in Ilford because my father had been given (in the mistaken supposition that he would want to proselytize a Jewish neighborhood) a church in Shoreditch that had no vicarage and no local congregation. Ilford, though in Essex, was then at the eastern extremity of London; its own western end was still country, though rapidly being "developed" into monotonous row upon row of small "mock-Tudor" houses I early learned to despise as jerry-built architectural monstrosities.

I didn't go to school, nor had my sister (nine years older) done so except briefly, another thing which set our household apart from others. Dissatisfied with my sister's one year at a convent boarding school during my infancy, and unimpressed by local day-schools (private and council), my mother, who had been teaching at a Constantinople high school run by the Church of Scotland when she met my father in 1910, taught me herself until at 12, enamored of the de Basil Russian Ballet to which my sister had taken me, I began daily classes at a school of ballet on the other side of London. At that point I was put on my honor to continue reading some history, and went also for weekly French, piano, and art lessons in London; my other formal education ceased.

Romantic and beautiful Wanstead and Valentines parks, frequent expeditions into the Essex countryside with my sister, and my mother's very strong sense of history, developed in me a taste for seeking-out and exploring the vanishing traces of the village Ilford which London had engulfed. The reading I did myself, and the reading aloud which was a staple of our family life, combined to give me a passion for England – for the nuances of country things, hedges and old churches and the names of wildflowers – even though part of me knew I was an outsider. Among Jews a Goy, among Gentiles (secular or Christian) a Jew or at least a ½ Jew (which was good or bad according to their degree of anti-Semitism), among Anglo-Saxons a Celt, in Wales a Londoner who not only did not speak Welsh but was not imbued with Welsh attitudes; among school children a strange exception whom they did not know whether to envy or mistrust – all of these anomalies predicated my later experience: I so often feel English, or perhaps European, in the United States, while in England I sometimes feel American – and certainly as a poet have been thought of for decades an American, for it was in the United States that I developed, though my first book had been published in England before I crossed the Atlantic. But though I was quick to scornfully protest anti-semitic remarks, or references to the Welsh language as a 'dialect', these feelings of not-belonging were positive, for me, not negative (except that I would have liked to learn Welsh and was too lazy to do so). I was given such a sense of confidence by my family, *in* my family, that though I was often shy (and have remained so in certain respects) I nevertheless experienced the sense of difference as an honor, as a part of knowing (secretly) from an early age – perhaps by seven, certainly before I was ten –

that I was an artist-person and had a destiny. I did not experience competitiveness, because I was alone. The age gap – nine years – between me and my sister was such that my childhood was largely that of an only child. I was given a great deal of freedom to roam about outdoors as soon as I'd learned to cross streets safely; only the loneliest depths of Wanstead Park were out of bounds. The house was full of books, many of them late seventeenth- and eighteenth-century volumes. Everyone in the family did some kind of writing; my mother and sister always seemed to be helping my father correct galley proofs. My mother sang *Lieder*, my sister was a really fine pianist. The church services I attended were, despite the frequent childish embarrassment I've mentioned and my teenage doubts, beautiful with candlelight and music, incense and ceremony and stained glass, the incomparable rhythms of the King Jame Bible and the Book of Common Prayer.

All of this sounds idealized *ad nauseam*, I'm afraid. There were also tremendous domestic arguments and periodic full-scale "rows" and even real tragedy (my gifted but erratic sister's life and her conflicts and reconciliations with my parents were complex). But all in all I did grow up in an extraordinarily rich environment which nurtured the imaginative, language-oriented potential I believe was an inherited gift; and gave me – or almost seduced me into – an appreciation of solitude which, since writing poetry is so essentially a solitary occupation, has always stood me in good stead and which perhaps I would not have developed if I'd gone to school (unless I'd *hated* school, of course) for I have a sociable, gregarious tendency too, that might have taken away too much time and concentration and necessary daydreaming. Or I might have become caught up in aggressive competition, to the certain detriment of my creative possibilities.

While it is true that I was not competitive because I had no peers to compete with (my playmates, whether neighbors or kids I met in the Park, were altogether separate from my beginnings in literature) I did, once I'd read Keats's letters, have hopes of Fame; but I thought of this as posthumous, and thus was saved from careerist ambition. And misinterpreting, to some extent, the gist of Mann's *Tonio Kröger*, I rather luxuriated in the protagonist's wistful alienation – though it was really his friend Lisaveta Ivanovna, the painter, the artist who was getting on with *doing her art*, who most excited me; especially since when I first read the story at 13, I had the *hutzpa* to believe I would be a painter as well as a poet. (I never deeply believed I would be a dancer despite the five years of my life when I took two ballet classes a day, shedding many tears in the process.)

Though my favorite poets were all men, I had enough faith in myself, or more precisely enough awe at the magic I knew sometimes worked through me, not to worry about that. Boys seemed, in fiction, to have more adventures; but in the "pretend-games" I made up and got my sister to play with me in my later childhood, some daring young female spies and messengers worked to combat Fascism and Nazism and to assist the government side in the Spanish Civil War (which was then going on). I didn't suppose my gender to be an obstacle to anything I really wanted to do.

Humanitarian politics came into my life early – seeing my father on a soapbox protesting Mussolini's invasion of Abyssinia; my father and sister both on soap-boxes protesting Britain's lack of support for Spain; my mother canvassing long before those events for the League of Nations Union; and all three of them working on behalf of German and Austrian refugees from 1933 onwards. When I was 11 and 12, unknown to my parents (who would have felt, despite their liberal views, that it was *going too far*, and was inappropriate for my age, as indeed it was) I used to sell the *Daily Worker* house-to-house in the working-class streets off Ilford Lane, down towards Barking, on Saturday mornings. Oddly enough I was never questioned, despite kneesocks and long plaits (or pigtails, as one said then) though I had many a door slammed in my face.

I've written only about my childhood, and not at all about the rest of my life and all its experiences of people, places, events; nothing about the mind's later journeys in literature and the other arts which mean so much to me; nothing about "intellectual stance", aesthetics, philosophy, religion. But there is, after all, no mystery about all of that: it's either in my poems or of little interest beyond the merely anecdotal; and in any case, this is an introductory essay, not a book. All that has taken place in my life since – all, that is, that has any bearing on my life as a poet – was in some way foreshadowed then. I am surprised to sound so deterministic, and I don't mean to suggest that the course of every life is inexorably set, genetically or by childhood experiences, for better or worse; nor that my own life had no options. Possibly I might have been a better person, and certainly a more efficient one in several respects, if I'd had a more disciplined and methodical education, more experience of economic struggle (never rich, and not extravagant, our household nevertheless never lacked for anything) and had not so early felt a sense of vocation and dedication to the art of poetry. But since I *did* have a vocation, to which some interesting genes contributed, it seems to me that I was fortunate in an upbringing favorable to their development; and this strongly affected my response to subsequent events and opportunities.

Poets owe to Poetry itself a loyalty which may at times be in conflict with the demands of domestic or other aspects of life. Out of those conflicts, sometimes, poetry itself re-emerges. For example, the impulse to reconcile what one believes to be necessary to one's human integrity, such as forms of political action, with the necessities of one's inner life, including its formal, aesthetic dynamic, motivates the attempt to write engaged or "political" poetry that is truly poetry, magnetic and sensuous, – the synthesis Neruda said was the most difficult of any to attain (but which our strange and difficult times cry out for). Yet sometimes the poems one is able to write and the needs and possibilities of day to day life remain separate from each other. One is in despair over the current manifestation of malevolent imbecility and the seemingly invincible power of rapacity, yet finds oneself writing a poem about the trout lilies in the spring woods. And one has promised to speak at a meeting or help picket a building. If one is conscientious, the only solution is to attempt to weigh conflicting claims at each crucial moment, and in general to try to juggle well and keep all the oranges dancing in the air at once.

DENISE LEVERTOV

## The Sun Going Down upon Our Wrath

You who are so beautiful—
your deep and childish faces,
your tall bodies—

Shall I warn you?

Do you know
what it was to have
a certitude of grasses waving
upon the earth though all
humankind were dust?
Of dust returning
to fruitful dust?

Do you already know
what hope is fading from us
and pay no heed,
see the detested grave-worm shrivel,
the once-despised,
and not need it?

Is there an odyssey
your feet pull you towards
away from now to walk
the waters, the fallen
orchard stars?
                    It seems
your fears are only the old fears, antique
anxieties, how graceful;
they lay as cloaks on shoulders
of men long dead,
skirts of sorrow wrapped
over the thighs of legendary women.

Can you be warned?

If you are warned will your beauty
scale off, to leave
gaping meat livid with revulsion?

No, who can believe it.
Even I in whose heart
stones rattle, rise each day
to work and imagine.

Get wisdom, get understanding, saith
the ancient. But he believed
there is nothing new under the sun,
his future
rolled away in great coils forever
into the generations.
Among conies the grass
grew again
and among bones.
And the bones would rise.

If there is time to warn you,
if you believed there shall be
never again a green blade in the crevice,
luminous eyes in rockshadow:
if you were warned and believed
the warning,

would your beauty
break into spears of fire,

fire to turn fire, a wall
of refusal, could there be
a reversal I cannot

hoist myself high enough
to see,
plunge myself deep enough
to know?

## The Jacob's Ladder

The stairway is not
a thing of gleaming strands
a radiant evanescence
for angels' feet that only glance in their tread, and need not
touch the stone.

It is of stone.
A rosy stone that takes
a glowing tone of softness
only because behind it the sky is a doubtful, a doubting
night gray.

A stairway of sharp
angles, solidly built.
One sees that the angels must spring
down from one step to the next, giving a little
lift of the wings:

and a man climbing
must scrape his knees, and bring
the grip of his hands into play. The cut stone
consoles his groping feet. Wings brush past him.
The poem ascends.


## The Mutes

Those groans men use
passing a woman on the street
or on the steps of the subway

to tell her she is a female
and their flesh knows it,

are they a sort of tune,
an ugly enough song, sung
by a bird with a slit tongue

but meant for music?

Or are they the muffled roaring
of deafmutes trapped in a building that is
slowly filling with smoke?

Perhaps both.

Such men most often
look as if groan were all they could do,
yet a woman, in spite of herself,

knows it's a tribute:
if she were lacking all grace
they'd pass her in silence:

so it's not only to say she's
a warm hole. It's a word

in grief-language, nothing to do with
primitive, not an ur-language;
language stricken, sickened, cast down

in decrepitude. She wants to
throw the tribute away, dis-
gusted, and can't,

it goes on buzzing in her ear,
it changes the pace of her walk,
the torn posters in echoing corridors

spell it out, it
quakes and gnashes as the train comes in.
Her pulse sullenly

had picked up speed,
but the cars slow down and
jar to a stop while her understanding

keeps on translating:
'Life after life after life goes by

without poetry,
without seemliness,
without love.'

## The Ache of Marriage

The ache of marriage:

thigh and tongue, beloved,
are heavy with it,
it throbs in the teeth

We look for communion
and are turned away, beloved,
each and each

It is leviathan and we
in its belly
looking for joy, some joy
not to be known outside it

two by two in the ark of
the ache of it.


## Fragrance of Life, Odor of Death

All the while among
the rubble even, and in
the hospitals, among the wounded,
                    not only beneath
                    lofty clouds

                        in temples
                    by the shores of lotus-dreaming
                    lakes

a fragrance:
flowers, incense, the earth-mist rising
of mild daybreak in the delta – good smell
of life.

It's in America
where no bombs ever
have screamed down smashing
the buildings, shredding the people's bodies,

tossing the fields of Kansas or Vermont or Maryland into the air
to land wrong way up, a gash of earth-guts . . .
it's in America, everywhere, a faint seepage,
I smell death.

[Hanoi-Boston-Maine, November 1972]


**Life at War**


The disasters numb within us
caught in the chest, rolling
in the brain like pebbles. The feeling
resembles lumps of raw dough

weighing down a child's stomach on baking day.
Or Rilke said it, 'My heart . . .
Could I say of it, it overflows
with bitterness . . . but no, as though

its contents were simply balled into
formless lumps, thus
do I carry it about.'
The same war

continues.
We have breathed the grits of it in, all our lives,
our lungs are pocked with it,
the mucous membrane of our dreams
coated with it, the imagination
filmed over with the gray filth of it:

the knowledge that humankind,

delicate Man, whose flesh
responds to a caress, whose eyes
are flowers that perceive the stars,

whose music excels the music of birds,
whose laughter matches the laughter of dogs,
whose understanding manifests designs
fairer than the spider's most intricate web,

still turns without surprise, with mere regret
to the scheduled breaking open of breasts whose milk
runs out over the entrails of still-alive babies,
transformation of witnessing eyes to pulp-fragments,
implosion of skinned penises into carcass-gulleys.

We are the humans, men who can make;
whose language imagines *mercy*,
*lovingkindness*; we have believed one another
mirrored forms of a God we felt as good—

who do these acts, who convince ourselves
it is necessary; these acts are done
to our own flesh; burned human flesh
is smelling in Viet Nam as I write.

Yes, this is the knowledge that jostles for space
in our bodies along with all we
go on knowing of joy, of love;

our nerve filaments twitch with its presence
day and night,
nothing we say has not the husky phlegm of it in the saying,
nothing we do has the quickness, the sureness,
the deep intelligence living at peace would have.


### Talk in the Dark

We live in history, says one.
We're flies on the hide of Leviathan, says another.

Either way, says one,
fears and losses.

And among losses, says another,
the special places our own roads were to lead to.

Our deaths, says one.
That's right, says another,
now it's to be a mass death.

Mass graves, says one, are nothing new.
No, says another, but this time there'll be no graves,
all the dead will lie where they fall.

Except, says one, those that burn to ash.
And are blown in the fiery wind, says another.

How can we live in this fear? says one.
From day to day, says another.

I still want to see, says one,
where my own road's going.

I want to live, says another, but where can I live
if the world is gone?


## The Task


As if God were an old man
always upstairs, sitting about
in sleeveless undershirt, asleep,
arms folded, stomach rumbling,
his breath from open mouth
strident, presaging death . . .

No, God's in the wilderness next door
—that huge tundra room, no walls and a sky roof—
busy at the loom. Among the berry bushes,
rain or shine, that loud clacking and whirring,
irregular but continuous;
God is absorbed in work, and hears
the spacious hum of bees, not the din,
and hears far-off
our screams. Perhaps
listens for prayers in that wild solitude.
And hurries on with the weaving:
till it's done, the great garment woven,
our voices, clear under the familiar
        blocked-out clamor of the task,
can't stop their

              terrible beseeching. God
imagines it sifting through, at last, to music
in the astounded quietness, the loom idle,
the weaver at rest.


## A Tree Telling of Orpheus

White dawn. Stillness.        When the rippling began
      I took it for sea-wind, coming to our valley with rumors
      of salt, of treeless horizons. But the white fog
didn't stir; the leaves of my brothers remained outstretched,
unmoving.
                  Yet the rippling drew nearer—and then
my own outermost branches began to tingle, almost as if
fire had been lit below them, too close, and their twig-tips
were drying and curling.
                              Yet I was not afraid, only
                  deeply alert.


I was the first to see him, for I grew
            out on the pasture slope, beyond the forest.
He was a man, it seemed: the two
moving stems, the short trunk, the two
arm-branches, flexible, each with five leafless
                                    twigs at their ends,
and the head that's crowned by brown or gold grass,
bearing a face not like the beaked face of a bird,
      more like a flower's.
                                    He carried a burden made of
some cut branch bent while it was green,
strands of a vine tight-stretched across it. From this,
when he touched it, and from his voice
which unlike the wind's voice had no need of our
leaves and branches to complete its sound,
                                    came the ripple.
But it was now no longer a ripple (he had come near and
stopped in my first shadow) it was a wave that bathed me
            as if rain
                  rose from below and around me
            instead of falling.
And what I felt was no longer a dry tingling:

I seemed to be singing as he sang, I seemed to know
what the lark knows; all my sap
            was mounting towards the sun that by now
                    had risen, the mist was rising, the grass
was drying, yet my roots felt music moisten them
deep under earth.


            He came still closer, leaned on my trunk:
            the bark thrilled like a leaf still-folded.
Music! There was no twig of me not
                        trembling with joy and fear.


Then as he sang
it was no longer sounds only that made the music:
he spoke, and as no tree listens I listened, and language
                    came into my roots
                                out of the earth,
                    into my bark
                            out of the air,
                    into the pores of my greenest shoots
                            gently as dew
and there was no word he sang but I knew its meaning.
He told of journeys,
            of where sun and moon go while we stand in dark,
        of an earth-journey he dreamed he would take some day
deeper than roots . . .
He told of the dreams of man, wars, passions, griefs,
            and I, a tree, understood words—ah, it seemed
my thick bark would split like a sapling's that
                            grew too fast in the spring
when a late frost wounds it.


                        Fire he sang,
that trees fear, and I, a tree, rejoiced in its flames.
New buds broke forth from me though it was full summer.
        As though his lyre (now I knew its name)
        were both frost and fire, its chords flamed
up to the crown of me.


            I was seed again.
                I was fern in the swamp.
                    I was coal.

And at the heart of my wood
(so close I was to becoming man or a god)
       there was a kind of silence, a kind of sickness,
           something akin to what men call boredom,
                            something
(the poem descended a scale, a stream over stones)
           that gives to a candle a coldness
                in the midst of its burning, he said.


It was then,
          when in the blaze of his power that
                  reached me and changed me
      I thought I should fall my length,
that the singer began
             to leave me.     Slowly
          moved from my noon shadow
                  to open light,
words leaping and dancing over his shoulders
back to me
          rivery sweep of lyre-tones becoming
slowly again
      ripple.


And I
        in terror
           but not in doubt of
                  what I must do
in anguish, in haste,
           wrenched from the earth root after root,
the soil heaving and cracking, the moss tearing asunder—
and behind me the others: my brothers
forgotten since dawn. In the forest
they too had heard,
and were pulling their roots in pain
out of a thousand years' layers of dead leaves,
      rolling the rocks away,
              breaking themselves
                    out of
                    their depths.
You would have thought we would lose the sound of the lyre,
          of the singing
so dreadful the storm-sounds were, where there was no storm,
        no wind but the rush of our

branches moving, our trunks breasting the air.
               But the music!
                              The music reached us.

Clumsily,
         stumbling over our own roots,
                              rustling our leaves
                                        in answer,
we moved, we followed.

All day we followed, up hill and down.
                              We learned to dance,
for he would stop, where the ground was flat,
                              and words he said
taught us to leap and to wind in and out
around one another       in figures       the lyre's measure designed.
The singer
         laughed till he wept to see us, he was so glad.
                                        At sunset
we came to this place I stand·in, this knoll
with its ancient grove that was bare grass then.
         In the last light of that day his song became
farewell.
         He stilled our longing.
         He sang our sun-dried roots back into earth,
watered them: all-night rain of music so quiet
                              we could almost
               not hear it in the
                         moonless dark.
By dawn he was gone.
               We have stood here since,
in our new life.    ( Heaven ? )
                'We have waited.
                              He does not return.
It is said he made his earth-journey, and lost
what he sought.
               It is said they felled him
and cut up his limbs for firewood.
                              And it is said
his head still sang and was swept out to sea singing.
Perhaps he will not return.
                         But what we have lived
comes back to us.

We see more.
                        We feel, as our rings increase,
something that lifts our branches, that stretches our furthest
                                                    leaf-tips
further.
        The wind, the birds,
                        do not sound poorer but clearer,
recalling our agony, and the way we danced.
The music!


## St Peter and the Angel


Delivered out of raw continual pain,
smell of darkness, groans of those others
to whom he was chained—

unchained, and led
past the sleepers,
door after door silently opening—
out!
        And along a long street's
majestic emptiness under the moon:

one hand on the angel's shoulder, one
feeling the air before him,
eyes open but fixed . . .

And not till he saw the angel had left him,
alone and free to resume
the ecstatic, dangerous, wearisome roads of
what he had still to do,
not till then did he recognize
this was no dream. More frightening
than arrest, than being chained to his warders:
he could hear his own footsteps suddenly.
Had the angel's feet
made any sound? He could not recall.
No one had missed him, no one was in pursuit.
He himself must be
the key, now, to the next door,
the next terrors of freedom and joy.

## Death Psalm: O Lord of Mysteries

She grew old.
She made ready to die.
She gave counsel to women and men, to young girls and young boys.
She remembered her griefs.
She remembered her happinesses.
She watered the garden.
She accused herself.
She forgave herself.
She learned new fragments of wisdom.
She forgot old fragments of wisdom.
She abandoned certain angers.
She gave away gold and precious stones.
She counted-over her handkerchiefs of fine lawn.
She continued to laugh on some days, to cry on others,
                    unfolding the design of her identity.
She practiced the songs she knew, her voice
                                gone out of tune
                    but the breathing-pattern perfected.
She told her sons and daughters she was ready.
She maintained her readiness.
She grew very old.
She watched the generations increase.
She watched the passing of seasons and years.
She did not die.

She did not die but lies half-speechless, incontinent,
                    aching in body, wandering in mind
                    in a hospital room.
A plastic tube, taped in her nose,
          disappears into one nostril.
Plastic tubes are attached to veins in her arms.
Her urine runs through a tube into a bottle under the bed.
On her back and ankles are black sores.
The black sores are parts of her that have died.
The beat of her heart is steady.
She is not whole.

She made ready to die, she prayed, she made her peace,
          she read daily from the lectionary.

She tended the green garden she had made,
    she fought off the destroying ants,
    she watered the plants daily
    and took note of their blossoming.
She gave sustenance to the needy.
She prepared her life for the hour of death.
But the hour has passed and she has not died.

O Lord of mysteries, how beautiful is sudden death
    when the spirit vanishes
    boldly and without casting
    a single shadowy feather of hesitation
    onto the felled body.

O Lord of mysteries, how baffling, how clueless
  is laggard death, disregarding
  all that is set before it
    in the dignity of welcome—
  laggard death, that steals
    insignificant patches of flesh—
  laggard death, that shuffles
  past the open gate,
  past the open hand,
  past the open,
        ancient,
        courteously waiting life.


## '. . . That Passeth All Understanding'


An awe so quiet
I don't know when it began.

A gratitude
had begun
to sing in me.

Was there
some moment
dividing
song from no song?

When does dewfall begin?

When does night
fold its arms over our hearts
to cherish them?

When is daybreak?


## Living

The fire in leaf and grass
so green it seems
each summer the last summer.

The wind blowing, the leaves
shivering in the sun,
each day the last day.

A red salamander
so cold and so
easy to catch, dreamily

moves his delicate feet
and long tail. I hold
my hand open for him to go.

Each minute the last minute.


## Passage

The spirit that walked upon the face of the waters
walks the meadow of long grass;
green shines to silver where the spirit passes.

Wind from the compass points, sun at meridian,
these are forms the spirit enters,
breath, *ruach*, light that is witness and by which we witness.

The grasses numberless, bowing and rising, silently
cry hosanna as the spirit
moves them and moves burnishing

over and again upon mountain pastures
a day of spring, a needle's eye
space and time are passing through like a swathe of silk.

# ELIZABETH JENNINGS

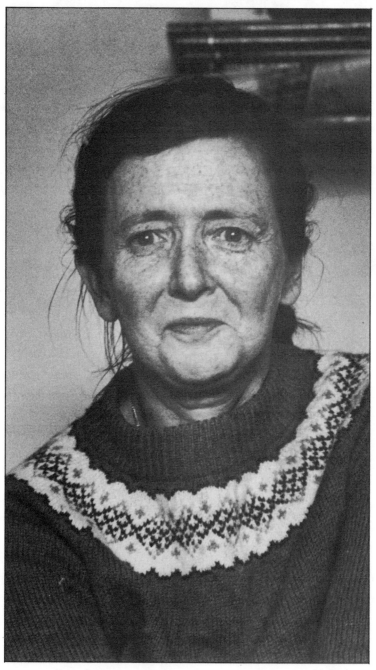

**Elizabeth Jennings** was born in 1926 in Boston, Lincolnshire. She went to school and university in Oxford, where she has lived for most of her life. In 1953 her first collection, *Poems*, was published by Oxford's Fantasy Press. A traditionalist in her verse technique, she was adopted by Robert Conquest for The Movement, but she is essentially a lyric poet, and has published an important book on mystical poetry, *Every Changing Shape* (1961).

She won a Somerst Maugham Award for her second book of poems, *A Way of Looking* (1955), and this enabled her to travel to Italy. During the next ten years she became a prolific poet but also suffered from ill health. She published many collections, including *A Sense of the World* (1958), *Song for a Birth or a Death* (1961), *Recoveries* (1964), *The Mind has Mountains* (1966), and *Collected Poems* (1967). Her *Selected Poems* appeared in 1979 from Carcanet, who have published all four of her recent collections: *Growing Points* (1975), *Consequently I Rejoice* (1977), *Moments of Grace* (1979) and *Celebrations and Elegies* (1982).

I distrust the kind of self-examination that leads you to expose what you think you know about yourself, but also – and this is much more serious – it makes you self-conscious about your work and turns you too obviously inwards to that darkness which I do not believe is our true concern in this life. I say 'in this life' because I am a believing Roman Catholic, but do not think I am neatly labelling myself and then moving on to other matters. Bearing the name of a great religion implies a truly terrible responsibility towards others, towards this suffering planet, towards our panicking apprehension of a cosmic disaster.

I have been a Catholic all my life but that does not mean I have never had doubts or difficulties, never questioned basic tenets of my faith. I do not want to enlarge in too great detail about this because by doing so I would be falling into the same trap or pitfall I inveighed against in my opening paragraph.

Any belief *does* demand a looking inward but that perusal is for examining your conscience not your identity. I would rather follow the great saint and philosopher, Thomas Aquinas, who as a child asked '*What* is God?' Like almost everyone who has some sort of fairly firm set of dogmas to affirm, I did when I was about fourteen start having difficulties (I was still a child in all ways and, therefore, a very late developer). My first sudden question to myself was 'What is the Holy Ghost?' (a Holy Spirit which Catholics wisely prefer to call the Third Person of the Blessed Trinity). I had never heard of Hopkins but I did imagine the Holy Spirit as an enormous bird with wings constantly spread wide. From the day of that pretty basic question, I moved on to almost every other kind of query about my creed.

It may be asked, 'Why am I detailing all this?' I am doing so, as briefly as possible, because I think it is important to my poetry. A deeply held belief is bound to influence all you do, and therefore all that you write. It was at about this time that I began to write very bad verse, though, of course, I did not think that at the time! But this verse never, then, expressed my religious worries. It was, perhaps, almost an escape for my troubled questioning, but never only that.

But enough of this. What I feel about writing poetry and have felt for a very long time is well expressed in Hopkins's sonnet 'As kingfishers catch fire . . .':

Crying *What I do is me: for that I came.*

I say more: the just man justices;
Keeps grace: that keeps all his goings graces;
Acts in God's eye what in God's eye he is—

'What I do is me' is really existentialism. For me my poetry is *me*, justifies my existence.

Although I had had early work published in *Oxford Poetry* and in London journals such as the *New English Weekly*, *Spectator*, *Poetry Review* and that great encourager of young talent, *Outposts*, my first book did not appear until I was twenty-seven. Today I can see it fairly objectively. There was a clear lyrical music and a certain mastery of form. My influences had been Auden, Edwin Muir, and Robert Graves and, of course, the great lyrical tradition since Shakespeare. My second book, *A Way of Looking*, marked a true turning-point in my life for I was lucky enough to win the Somerset Maugham Award for it, which meant spending three months abroad, most of that in Rome.

Rome was more than a revelation to me. You need to spend some time there to absorb its special flavour, to learn its spirit of place. If you are a Catholic, you soon realise what a Catholic city is like, even though the behaviour of many Italian Roman Catholics is far from edifying, especially that of the young and the married men. The former think nothing of trying to pick you up in church, while the latter often seem to think that as long as their wives and children go to Mass and the Sacraments, they themselves will have a passport to heaven! Yet in spite of this, you do feel that in this great centre of Christianity that faith is truly being lived. Italians believe fervently even when they do not practise their religion regularly. In short, Rome contains either very good or very bad Catholics.

How did this affect me? It did nothing less than bring my religion alive, take away the puritanical fear I had acquired in England and release my imagination.

I have always written poetry. It is quite literally a way of life. Once or twice I have feared, and even felt more than sure, that the fountain had dried; I have always been wrong. Like most poets I have suffered from bad reviews, though I have also sometimes learnt something useful from critical ones.

I write reviews of prose books, and articles, and I have written books about poetry for children and others. I think that the better a poet is, the finer and more illuminating and lively their prose tends to be: think of Keats's and Hopkins's letters or the critical writing of Eliot and Auden.

I owe debts to many poets and many friends for reading my work and for giving me time to write. Gratitude is a virtue which, along with steadfastness, I value above all others. I hope I shall always do so.

ELIZABETH JENNINGS

## Almost Drowning

First there was coming,
A coming-to, a sense of giddy
Limbs, another's or wings gleaming
Across the light. I was the body.
Was air or earth unsteady?

Second were voices,
Syllables, vowels were turning, running
Together. I was having races
With these, to overtake their meaning.
Then one word about drowning.

Third was the sea,
The tear of it about me still,
The time in it never to be
Within my compass or my will,
A birth or death writ small.


## Invocation and Incantation

I caught a night-bird on a shaft of wind.
I thought and found it sleeping in my mind.

I took a leaf and held it in my palm.
It sent no shiver through me but pure calm.

I went out late at night to taste the air.
A star shone back at me like my own prayer.

Each second someone's born, another dies
But early hours do not contain their cries.

Sleepers are all about. O let them see,
When they wake up, peace garnered now for me

And may they lay their sleep upon my mind—
A bird with folded wings no nightmares find.

## Fragment for the Dark

Let it not come near me, let it not
Fold round or over me. One weak hand
Clutches a foot of air, asks the brisk buds
To suffer grey winds, spear through
Fog I feel in me. Give me the magic
To see grounded starlings, their polish
As this threat of all-day night. Mind, mind
In me, make thoughts candles to light me
Out of the furthest reach of possible nights.
Lantern me, stars, if I look up through wet hands,
Show assurance in blurred shining. I have
Put every light in the house on.
May their filaments last till true morning.


## Star Midnight

Isn't the sky wider, isn't the air
Steeper, the stars more preening,
Isn't the mind climbing stair by stair
And gradually winning
Advantage over earth, earning the clear
Precisest meaning?

Summer suggests this or its evenings do
When stars break through the warm
Darkness. The bare hand stretches out to strew
A bracelet from its arm
And the mind is sure that it has caught the true
Ultimate calm.

A moth flits by. A cat calls out. The intent
Moment is held. An hour
Pours out not in bell-notes but by the consent
Of purest thought. Say prayer
Or say this is a settled argument,
Say we are near

Knowing beyond discoveries with names
Or theories, but worldly-wise
In ways astonishing beyond our dreams
Yet here before our eyes.
I take a star down and the air still gleams
More in those skies.


## A Child in the Night

The child stares at the stars. He does not know
Their names. He does not care. Time halts for him
And he is standing on the earth's far rim
As all the sky surrenders its bright show.

He will not feel like this again until
He falls in love. He will not be possessed
By dispossession till he has caressed
A face and in its eyes seen stars stand still.


## Hatching

His night has come to an end and now he must break
The little sky which shielded him. He taps
Once and nothing happens. He tries again
And makes a mark like lightning. He must thunder,
Storm and shake and break a universe
Too small and safe. His daring beak does this.

And now he is out in a world of smells and spaces.
He shivers. Any air is wind to him.
He huddles under wings but does not know
He is already shaping feathers for
A lunge into the sky. His solo flight
Will bring the sun upon his back. He'll bear it,
Carry it, learn the real winds, by instinct
Return for food and, larger than his mother,
Avid for air, harry her with his hunger.

## Instinct for Seasons

As some have divining instincts
For water, gold or diamond,
Can tell by a twitch or a scent,
So others, I among them,
Have a similar gift to tell
Of a season changing. It's not
In the power of one sense only
Or a habit of memory.
If I could tell the causes
I'd lose the knack or gift.

But causes jump to mind
And here are a few:—a concern
For how a bird's song hollows
A distance at early dawn
And climbs to a clarity
Which has something to do with the sun;
And again, the way the petals
Lift the face of a flower
Till it balances on the light
As a gull imposes its stillness
On a crest of impulsive wave.

All these explain but little.
Perhaps, though city-bred
(The house wasn't far from a town),
I have a farmer's feeling
Of when to plough or reap.
In the place where blood and the mind
Meet and are reconciled,
A recognition of seasons,
Days before they have come,
Leaps with a throb and a drive
And today exults with the sun
And did so before it arrived.

## For a Gentle Friend

I have come to where the deep words are
Spoken with care. There is no more to hide.
I toss away the cold stance of my fear

And move O far, far out to be beside
One who owns all language in extremes
Of death. We watch the coming-in now tide.

We have lived through the nightmares death presumes
To wound us with. We faced the darkest place.
Death the familiar enters all our rooms.

We wear its colour. Its mask's on our face.
But not for long. It's good to let tears run.
This is the quick, the nerve, also the grace

Of death. It brings our life into the sun
And we are grateful. Grief is gracious when
It takes the character of this kind one,

This gentle person. We re-live his life
And marvel at the quiet good he's done.

## Is It Dual-Natured?

Is it dual-natured to be so alive
Sometimes that your flesh seems far too small
To contain the power of the sun, or how stars thrive,

But then to be diminished, become a small
Dark of yourself, yourself your hiding-place
Where you converse with shadows which are tall

Or listen to low echoes with no grace
Of lyric joy or calm? I do not feel
Divided deep. Sometimes, the sense of the place

Where I am most light and eager can make me thrill
To the planet's course. I am pulled or do
I draw myself up, into the sun's overspill?

One or other. It only matters I know
What levitation would be and am grateful to learn
What's instinctive to birds is what makes the wind blow.

I will risk all extremes. I will flounder, will stumble, will burn.


## The One Drawback *key poem*

It stays, it stays. I have incalculable
Hours of supreme sun, light which always can
Draw me on, running with light, draw me on
In somebody else's plan
But the movement is my own.

I should expect dark to be given when
I have such lights, some are tall as the sun,
Others are hearths which friends will sit around.
When these lights have gone
I am drawn underground.

I wander there but break sometimes into
A run. I only tire myself, I wait,
Imagining summers of another world.
To move in dark is a fate
But I know also the gold

Dawns of the world outside me, and within
Dawns in which words break into fresh song,
My mind is raided by a dazzling light,
Sun is where I belong
But I'm an expert on night.

## In a Garden

When the gardener has gone this garden
Looks wistful and seems waiting an event.
It is so spruce, a metaphor of Eden
And even more so since the gardener went,

Quietly godlike, but, of course, he had
Not made me promise anything, and I
Had no one tempting me to make the bad
Choice. Yet I still felt lost and wonder why.

Even the beech tree from next door which shares
Its shadow with me, seemed a kind of threat.
Everything was too neat and someone cares

In the wrong way. I need not have stood long
Mocked by the smell of a mown lawn, and yet
I did. Sickness for Eden was so strong.


## Rembrandt's Late Self-Portraits

You are confronted with yourself. Each year
The pouches fill, the skin is uglier.
You give it all unflinchingly. You stare
Into yourself, beyond. Your brush's care
Runs with self-knowledge. Here

Is a humility at one with craft.
There is no arrogance. Pride is apart
From this self-scrutiny. You make light drift
The way you want. Your face is bruised and hurt
But there is still love left.

Love of the art and others. To the last
Experiment went on. You stared beyond
Your age, the times. You also plucked the past
And tempered it. Self-portraits understand,
And old age can divest,

With truthful changes, us of fear of death.
Look, a new anguish. There, the bloated nose,
The sadness and the joy. To paint's to breathe,
And all the darknesses are dared. You chose
What each must reckon with.

## Spell of the Elements

Fire and water, air and earth
Contend, unite. A magic birth
Is taking place somewhere not far
Celebrated by a star.

Take the music of the wind,
Take the fingers of a mind
Making, breaking, letting go.
Take the blanket of the snow

And a necklace of the stars,
Take the footsteps of the hours.
All can spell-bind, all can build,
All will come if you have called.

We are subject to a spell.
It is married to free-will.
Come the spring, the earth will lie
Lucky under lucky sky.

No determinism has
Power to hold us long. We pass
Into every element,
Come and gone but never spent.

*Jennings is not suicidal*
*Plath is compared to*
*Nick (wristed) Plath*

## A Chorus

Over the surging tides and the mountain kingdoms,
Over the pastoral valleys and the meadows,
Over the cities with their factory darkness,
Over the lands where peace is still a power,
Over all these and all this planet carries
A power broods, invisible monarch, a stranger
To some, but by many trusted. Man's a believer
Until corrupted. This huge trusted power
Is spirit. He moves in the muscle of the world,
In continual creation. He burns the tides, he shines
From the matchless skies. He is the day's surrender.
Recognize him in the eye of the angry tiger,
In the sigh of a child stepping at last into sleep,
In whatever touches, graces and confesses,
In hopes fulfilled or forgotten, in promises

Kept, in the resignation of old men—
This spirit, this power, this holder together of space
Is about, is aware, is working in your breathing.
But most he is the need that shows in hunger
And in the tears shed in the lonely fastness.
And in sorrow after anger.

## Fantasy

Tree without leaf I stand
Bird unfeathered cannot fly
I a beggar weep and cry
Not for coins but for a hand

To beg with. All my leaves are down,
Feathers flown and hand wrenched off
Bird and tree and beggar grown
Nothing on account of love.

## For a Child Born Dead

What ceremony can we fit
You into now? If you had come
Out of a warm and noisy room
To this, there'd be an opposite
For us to know you by. We could
Imagine you in lively mood

And then look at the other side,
The mood drawn out of you, the breath
Defeated by the power of death.
But we have never seen you stride
Ambitiously the world we know.
You could not come and yet you go.

But there is nothing now to mar
Your clear refusal of our world.
Not in our memories can we mould
You or distort your character.
Then all our consolation is
That grief can be as pure as this.

## The Animals' Arrival

So they came
Grubbing, rooting, barking, sniffing,
Feeling for cold stars, for stone, for some hiding-place,
Loosed at last from heredity, able to eat
From any tree or from ground, merely mildly themselves,
And every movement was quick, was purposeful, was proposed.
The galaxies gazed on, drawing in their distances.
The beasts breathed out warm on the air.

No one had come to make anything of this,
To move it, name it, shape it a symbol;
The huge creatures were their own depth, the hills
Lived lofty there, wanting no climber.
Murmur of birds came, rumble of underground beasts
And the otter swam deftly over the broad river.

There was silence too.
Plants grew in it, it wove itself, it spread, it enveloped
The evening as day-calls died and the universe hushed, hushed.
A last bird flew, a first beast swam
And prey on prey
Released each other
(Nobody hunted at all):
They slept for the waiting day.

## A Letter to Peter Levi

Reading your poems I am aware
Of translucencies, of birds hovering
Over estuaries, of glass being spun for huge domes.
I remember a walk when you showed me
A tablet to Burton who took his own life.
You seem close to fragility yet have
A steel-like strength. You help junkies,
You understand their language,
You show them the stars and soothe them.
You take near-suicides and talk to them,
You are on the strong side of life, yet also the brittle,
I think of blown glass sometimes but reject the simile.
Yet about your demeanour there is something frail,
The strength is within, won from simple things
Like swimming and walking.
Your pale face is like an ikon, yet
Any moment, any hour, you break to exuberance,
And then it is our world which is fragile:
You toss it like a juggler.

# ELAINE FEINSTEIN

**Elaine Feinstein** was born in Lancashire in 1930, and grew up in Leicestershire. After reading English at Newnham College, Cambridge, she read for the Bar, worked on the editorial staff of Cambridge University Press, and lectured in the literature department at the University of Essex. She now lives in Cambridge.

She has published five poetry books: *In a Green Eye* (Cape Goliard, 1966), *The Magic Apple Tree* (Hutchinson, 1971), *The Celebrants* (Hutchinson, 1973), *Some Unease and Angels: Selected Poems* (Hutchinson, 1977), and *The Feast of Eurydice* (Next Editions, 1980). Her *Selected Poems* of the Russian poet Marina Tsvetayeva was first published by Oxford University Press in 1971, and then issued in the Penguin Modern European Poets series in 1974; an expanded edition appeared from Oxford in 1981.

Her six novels include *Children of the Rose* (1975), *The Ecstasy of Dr Miriam Garner* (1976) *The Survivors* (1982), and *The Border* (1984).

Perhaps I was too much cherished as a child, because my mother could carry none of the children she conceived after me – she had rhesus negative blood – and my survival seemed miraculous. My father would have been indulgent in any case, I think; it was his temperament. As it was, all through my childhood I can remember his brown eyes, like those of a faithful dog, turned towards me with loving wonder. I used to enjoy inventing stories even before I was old enough to go to school. As he listened to them, his lips mouthed the words after mine. These things have their effect. An inner certainty of being loved and valued went a long way to create my own sense of resilience in later years spent in a world that felt altogether alien. I never altogether lost my childhood sense of being fortunate.

My father had left school at twelve himself, and had little patience with books or teachers. Really, he only believed in luck and hard work; that's how he coped with the ups and downs of a small business in the thirties. We were never rich, and often lived beyond our means. My mother's infinitely more urbane family saw my father as a hopeless optimist and a dreamer. So he was, and I loved him for it, along with his gentleness and his physical strength and his indomitable courage. I felt quite hostile to the Wyggeston School, to which my mother insisted I should be sent, since I understood their values opposed his.

It was my mother who determined that my schooling should be as good as Leicester could provide. I was grateful for that, though I doubt if I was a popular pupil. I was restless and constrained, and in all my years there never learnt how to accept school discipline. I was always in trouble for not having the right shoes, or forgetting my books, or pencils. Even my precocious quickness at reading meant that I spent a good deal of my first years at school fuming with impatience. I was not, however, a solitary child outside school.

I had eleven cousins also living in Leicester, and most weekends one or two would stay overnight with me. We explored wild patches of land, wired off and unbuilt-over; climbed trees; hid under redcurrant bushes; solemnly perfected bows and arrows. The war, when it began, hardly reached us; even the arrival of a timid young refugee girl from Germany (who was adopted by my parents for six or seven years), did nothing to dispel the absolute conviction of safety in which I moved. Just recently, tasting a stale Sunpat chocolate raisin from a London slot-machine I remembered again the illicit excitement we all felt rehearsing for an air-raid, and marvelled at my illusion of immunity.

That sense of security was exploded, once and for all, at the war's end, when I read what exactly had been done to so many children, as young as I was, in the Hell of Hitler's camps. You could say that in that year I became Jewish for the first time. That is not something I regret. But that appalling revelation of human cruelty towards ordinary people did me incalculable emotional damage. For a very long time afterwards, I could feel no ordinary human emotion without testing it against that imagined experience, and either suspecting it or dismissing it.

Of course, I went on reading. Indeed, it was about this time that I began to involve myself seriously in school work. I found very little effort was required to do quite well in most subjects, even unlikely ones like mathematics and science. I became competitive. But I remember knowing, even at the time, that I was working only with the topmost layer of my brain. With that straightforward, sequential layer I wrote competent essays, passed examinations, won an Open Exhibition to Newnham College, Cambridge. But for some years I wrote no poems.

A few years later, when I was married with two children, I began to start writing again. It was a particularly bleak time of my life. I was altogether unsuited to housewifely responsibility (though I have always been grateful that I took the risk of becoming a mother of three sons) and I could not make friends easily with the young women who lived round about me on the housing estate in Cambridge. And I was as much cut-off emotionally from the world round me as if I had been divided from it by glass. I didn't notice the seasons changing, or the trees in the garden. My mind felt white and bloodless. I was trying to write an academic piece on Katherine Mansfield in the few hours a day I had free from domestic chores; but somehow my mind wandered from that task and I began to scribble quite unrelated observations. And then, suddenly, I found that as soon as I tried to find words for the black shine of black trees in the rain, say, or the noise of heels knocking on a pavement at night, I could respond quite sharply to everything. Everything was after all *relevant* to me. It was like coming back to life. I began to take eager journal notes of whatever I noticed, taking great pains to describe things as cleanly and clearly as possible. Sometimes I tried to turn my notes into poems. But the finished poems were absolutely not the point in themselves. It was the *process* that seemed important to me, the attention I was able to give once again to people around me and my returning memories. I watched my children closely; called up a vision of my father at his saw bench; tried to catch the exultation of childbirth. And I began to read poetry again voraciously.

What did I want from poetry? First and foremost, I wanted poems that were genuinely trying to make sense of experience. But I wanted something else as well; not tight, knotty images, but plain propositions, lines that came singing out of the poem with a perfection of phrasing like lines of music. I found that, in American poets as different from one another as Ezra Pound and Wallace Stevens.

But finally, it was the poetry of another culture and another language, which did most to give a direction to own my personal poetry. I came upon the poetry of Marina Tsvetayeva more or less by accident. At the time I was lecturing in the literature department at the University of Essex. Reading Pasternak's *Safe Conduct* there, I came across a description of Tsvetayeva's verse, and the assertion that she was among the four great Russian poets of the century. To my surprise, I found she had not been translated, so I asked for help from Angela Livingstone of the same department, who made literal word-for-word translations of some of her most important poems for me, and with these and the Moscow-Leningrad edition of her poems which came out in 1966, I began to try to make versions of her work. They were poems made entirely for myself, with as much of a contemporary English voice as I could give them. They were first published in a very small literary magazine and I was very surprised when both Oxford University Press and Penguin decided to commission a book of them. By the time I had launched into that project, I had learnt enough of Tsvetayeva's life to be astonished at her stamina and courage, and to understand how much a part of her personal tragedy it was to be without books in Russia and without readers in the West.

Tsvetayeva was my teacher of courage. She opened the way to a wholeness of self-exposure which my English training would otherwise have made impossible. And it was not only my poetry she influenced. I began writing novels for the first time under her spell, allowing myself to say *not* what I knew was expected; *not* what my education had told me was appropriately serious; but everything that I truly felt, without trying for false authority and analysis. Since then I have written six novels as well as my books of poems. It is not so common these days for a writer to enjoy both genres; and, if pushed, I usually agree that I feel myself to be first and foremost a poet. If that shows in my novels, it is not because they are fancy, or decorated, but because I am habitually careful with language, and perhaps become elliptical in my desire for compression. One thing I am certain about, looking back over the last twenty years; I don't think I could have made sense of my life without writing about it.

ELAINE FEINSTEIN

## Calliope in the labour ward

she who has no love for women
married and housekeeping

now the bird notes begin
in the blood in the June morning
look how these ladies are
as little squeamish as
men in a great war

have come into their bodies
as their brain dwindles to
the silver circle on
eyelids under sun
and time opens
pain in the shallows to wave up and over them

grunting in gas and air
they sail to a
darkness without self
where no will reaches

in that abandon less
than human
give birth
bleak as a goddess

## Song of Power

For the baiting
children in my
son's school class who
say I am a witch:
black is the
mirror you give me

drawn inward at siege
sightless, mumbling:
criminal, to bear three
children like fruit
cannot be guarded
against enemies.

Should I have lived sterile?
The word returns me.
If any supernatural power
my strangeness earns me
I now invoke, for
all Gods are

anarchic even the Jews'
outside his own laws, with
his old name
confirms me, and I
call out for the
strange ones with wild hair

all the earth over to
make their own coherence
a fire their children
may learn to bear at last
and not burn in.


**Anniversary**


Suppose I took out a slender ketch from
under the spokes of Palace pier tonight to
catch a sea going fish for you

or dressed in antique goggles and wings and
flew down through sycamore leaves into the park

or luminescent through some planetary strike
put one delicate flamingo leg over the sill of your lab

Could I surprise you?      or would you insist on
keeping a pattern to link every transfiguration?

Listen, I shall have to whisper it
into your heart directly:      we are all
supernatural / every day
we rise new creatures / cannot be predicted

## By the Cam

Tonight I think this landscape could
      easily swallow me: I'm smothering
in marshland, wet leaves, brown
      creepers, puddled in
rain and mud, one little gulp and

I'll be gone without a splutter:
      into night, flood, November, rot and
river-scud. Scoopwheeled for drainage.
      And by winter, the fen will be brittle and
pure again, an odd, tough, red leaf frozen
      out of its year into the ice of the gutter.

## Patience

In water nothing is mean. The fugitive
enters the river, she is washed free;
her thoughts unravel like weeds of
green silk: she moves downstream
as easily as any cold-water creature

can swim between furred stones, brown
fronds, boots and tins the river holds equally.
The trees hiss overhead. She feels their shadows.
She imagines herself clean as a fish,
evasive, solitary, dumb. Her prayer:
to make peace with her own monstrous nature.

## Marriage

Is there ever a new beginning when every
word has its ten years' weight, can there be
what you call conversation between us?
Relentless you are as you push me
to dance and I lurch away from you
weeping, and yet can we bear to lie
silent under the ice together like
fish in a long winter?

A letter now from York is a reminder of
windless Rievaulx, the hillside moving through
limestone arches, in the ear's liquid the
whir of dove notes: we were a fellowship of three
strangers walking in northern brightness, our
searches peaceful, in our silence the
resonance of stones only, any celibate
could look for such retreat, for me
it was a luxury to be insisted on
in the sight of those grass-overgrown dormitories

We have taken our shape from the
damage we do one another, gently as
bodies moving together at night, we amend
our gestures, softly we hold our places:
in the alien school morning in the
small stones of your eyes I know how
you want to be rid of us, you were
never a family man, your virtue is
lost, even alikeness deceived us
love, our spirits sprawl together
and both at last are distorted

and yet we go toward birthdays and other
marks     not wryly     not thriftily
waiting, for where shall we find it, a
joyous, a various world? in fury
we share, which keeps us, without
resignation: tender whenever we touch     what
else we share     this flesh     we
bring together     it hurts to
think of dying as we lie close

## Dad

Your old hat hurts me, and those black
        fat raisins you liked to press into
my palm from your soft heavy hand:
        I see you staggering back up the path
with sacks of potatoes from some local farm,
        fresh eggs, flowers. Every day I grieve

for your great heart broken and you gone.
        You loved to watch the trees. This year
you did not see their Spring.
        The sky was freezing over the fen
as on that somewhere secretly appointed day
        you beached: cold, white-faced, shivering.

What happened, old bull, my loyal
        hoarse-voiced warrior? The hammer
blow that stopped you in your track
        and brought you to a hospital monitor
could not destroy your courage
        to the end you were
uncowed and unconcerned with pleasing anyone.

I think of you now as once again safely
        at my mother's side, the earth as
chosen as a bed, and feel most sorrow for
        all that was gentle in
my childhood buried there
        already forfeit, now forever lost.

## Coastline

This is the landscape of the Cambrian age:
        shale, blue quartz, planes of slate streaked with
iron and lead; soapstone, spars of calcite;
        in these pools, fish are the colour of sand,
velvet crabs like weeds, prawns transparent as water.

This shore was here before man. Every tide
    the sea returns, and floats the bladderwrack,
The flower animals swell and close over creatures
    rolled-in, nerveless, sea-food, fixed and forgotten.

My two thin boys balance on Elvan Stone
    bent-backed, intent, crouched with their string and pins,
their wet feet white, lips salt, and skin wind-brown,
    watching with curiosity and compassion:
further out, Time and Chance are waiting to happen.


## At the edge

### 1

In your delirium your eyelids were
    raisin brown, and your beard like wet straw.
We were washed in salt on the same pillow together
    and we watched the walls change level gently as water.

But now there are white drops at the window
    this morning, in grey light, your fever gone,
do you even remember the dance of words that
    slipped between us like fish? My sober love.

### 2

Behind your darkness and
marooned again: I know that
island, sisters, where you wait to
offer your magenta crenellations
to some explorer, unafraid of the moon.

Yet I would bless you with no
causewayside, no mainland even,
but only more silence for you to turn in
so you receive at last whatever
light your creole petals need to open.

3

Into sleet over
stones and shells
on a visit to Winchelsea
to that lake of wet sand and sky where
the red water runs
salt from
sun into sea,

we laughed
crunching over
snow pouches to leap
at the planet's periphery
but our cries
died about us:

we were
black points upon
too inhuman a canvas
and were dwindling fast.
It was not just the Ural wind
drove us
inland for shelter.


**Night thoughts**


Uncurtained, my long room floats on
    darkness, moored in rain,
my shelves of orange skillets
    lie out in the black grass.
Tonight I can already taste
    the wet soil of their ghosts.
And my spirit looks through the glass:
    I cannot hold on for ever.

No tenure, in garden trees, I
    hang like a leaf, and stare
at cartilaginous shapes
    my shadow their visitor.
And words cannot brazen it out.
    Nothing can hold for ever.

## The Medium

My answer would have to be music
which is always deniable, since in my
silence, which you question, is only a landscape

of water, old trees and a few irresolute
birds. The weather is also inconstant.
Sometimes the light is golden, the leaves unseasonable.

And sometimes the ice is red, and the moon
hangs over it, peeled, like a chinese fruit.
I am sorry not to be more articulate.

When I try, the words turn ugly as rats and
disorder everything, I cannot be quiet,
I want so much to be quiet and loving

If only you wanted that. My sharpest thoughts
wait like assassins always in the dry wheat. They
chat and grin. Perhaps you should talk to them?

## Sybil

The present holder of the papers sits
behind broken glass in the derelict warehouse
androgynous, black-skulled, and ricket-boned
grimacing to deride her visitors,

skinny, tobacco-stained, alert, she has
bartered her memories of
bark smells, wild
almonds and water plants to
taste the sour air of neglected cities.

Trembling with adrenalin of
indignation, like euphoria, she
licks her lips at the modern
crystal set in the wall. Look,

it is all happening again.

We can watch together
how terror smiles through the screen
like a handsome peasant with his violin.

She sits and nods and waits for
the latest obsequies, with
a squint eye and a slant hand, she
writes: beware this generation's prophecies.


*From* **The Feast of Eurydice**


1

    The dead are strong.
That winter as you wandered,
    the cold continued, still
the brightness cut
    my shape into the snow:
I would have let you go!

    Your mother blew
my dust into your lips
    a powder white as cocaine,
my name, runs to your nerves
    and now I move again in your song.
You will not let me go.

    The dead are strong.
Although in darkness I was lost
    and had forgotten all pain
long ago: in your song
    my lit face remains
and so we go

    over pools that crack
like glass, through forests shining
    black with twigs that wait
for you to wake them, I return
    in your praise, as Eurydice's
ghost I light the trees.

    The dead are strong.

3

A path of cinders, I remember,
    and limping upward
not yet uprooted from
    my dream, a ghost

with matted eyes, air-sacs
    rasping, white
brain, I staggered
    after you

Orpheus, when you first
    called, I pushed
the sweet earth from my mouth
    and sucked in

all the powders of volcanic ash
    to follow you
obedient    up
    that crumbling slope

to the very last ridge—
    where I saw clumps of
yellow camomile in the dunes
    and heard the applause

of your wild mother
    great Calliope
crying good, my son, good
    in the fumes of the crater.

When the wiring sputtered
    at my wedding feast
she was hectic, glittering;
    her Arabian glass

burst into darkness
    and her flesh shimmered.
She was still laughing, there,
    on that pumice edge

with all Apollo's day behind her
    as I saw your heavy
shoulders turn. Your lips move.
    Then your eyes.

and I lay choking    Orpheus
    what hurt    most then    was
your stunned face
    lost

cruel    never to be touched
    again, and watching
a blown leaf in your
    murderous eye

shrivel . . .

# RUTH FAINLIGHT

**Ruth Fainlight** has published nine books of poems, including *Cages* (1966) and *To See the Matter Clearly* (1968) from Macmillan; *The Region's Violence* (1973), *Another Full Moon* (1976), *Sibyls And Others* (1980) and *Fifteen to Infinity* (1983) from Hutchinson; and *Climates* (1983) from Bloodaxe. Her translation from the Portuguese of a selection of poems by Sophia de Mello Breyner is forthcoming from Black Swan Books.

Ruth Fainlight's mother was born in what was then a small town on the eastern borders of the Austro-Hungarian Empire and is now part of the Soviet Union, while her father was born in London, and she herself in New York City, in 1931. She has lived mostly in Britain from the age of 15, though she still retains her American citizenship.

My nearest approach to the clarity, calmness, and exultation of what
I understand as contemplation, has been through the process of
fixing my mind on the originating inspiration of a poem, and the
endeavour to express it. Like the speaker in my poem 'Introspection
of a Sibyl' I find out what I have to say by saying it in the only way I
can. Writing poetry is what I do to make contact with my spirit and
the spirits that inhabit me, and gain insight into those incoherent
aspects of myself that only poetry can deal with: the one sure aid to
understanding what compels me to write it.

But as well as being a method of self-examination and a technique
of contemplation, writing poems is a very effective method of getting
away from the agitations and demands of the self. T.S. Eliot wrote,
'Poetry is not a turning loose of emotion, but an escape from emotion;
it is not the expression of personality, but an escape from personality. But of course, only those who have personality and emotions
know what it means to want to escape from those things.'

With the passage of time I have gained certain insights, and
become more practised in manipulating the instruments of the
search: as though objectivity and fluency advanced hand in hand. I
cannot agree totally with A.E. Housman when he writes, 'Poetry is
not the thing said but a way of saying it . . .', but I know that the
challenge of language, the delight in words and recognition of
their vitality and power, are as important as the need for self-
expression.

Art is play – and one characteristic of play is that absolute
seriousness and absorption in the present shared by children and
artists, and which has nothing to do with necessity, utility, or duty.
Conditioning as a female has made it very hard to retain, to
acknowledge, or to nurture, the child-like part of my nature. In our
culture (that amalgamation of Graeco-Roman/Judeo-Christian beliefs
and values), woman is made the custodian and prisoner of the realm
of matter, the "grown-up" one who deals with practical quotidian
reality, while the metaphysical worlds of fantasy and intellect and
spirit, and all the games of life, from war to physics, have been seen as
the privileged domain of men. But, 'Except ye become as little
children, ye shall not enter into the kingdom of heaven.'

St Teresa said, 'To be a woman is to feel your wings droop.' A
specifically female anger has been the impetus for many of my
poems. Nevertheless, I am convinced that the 'negative capability' of
the poet extends beyond/below/above gender. I am a poet who is a
woman, not a woman poet.

To be a poet: which means resisting any temptation that might
divert energy or distract attention from the necessary passive alert-

ness – like that of a resting hound – to the first stirrings of a poem, never to set up barriers against the Muse. Marina Tsvetayeva expressed this in her essay 'Art in the Light of Conscience' as, '. . . the highest degree of subjection to that visitation – one; control of that visitation – two. The highest degree of being mentally cleft open and highest of – activity.' The worst temptation is to ignore those intimations, those signals, as though testing their power and persistence; or perhaps it is a case of challenging my own powers: the sin of pride, as expressed in 'As Though She Were A Sister'.

The problem of the Muse: Is she mother, sister, lover, oneself? Easy enough for a man to project the anima outward, but the animus, as is implicit in the more general use of the word to denote a hostile reaction, can become a repressive manifestation that muffles and paralyses with self-doubt. It took me a long time to understand that my poem 'The Other' is about the Muse.

Where does my work come from? I think there is an almost continual monologue or soliloquy inside my head: a voice commenting on what I see and feel and explaining it to me, mulling over preoccupations of perhaps years' duration, sometimes even making jokes. And at irregular intervals, a phrase or group of words will demand attention, like a branch tapping against the window or a child tugging at my skirt. This is what I am always waiting for, and every time, it seems a miracle.

These words have a particular tune, which is the ground-rhythm of the poem presenting itself, and through all subsequent work and revision I must be faithful to that melody. Usually it starts in my head, anywhere and at any time, and I hurry to find a pencil and scrap of paper to record the vital phrase. But sometimes it will happen when I am writing in my notebook, or answering a letter from a friend. Then I notice the language I am using seems to have changed, and realise I have written down the phrase that will initiate a poem.

This phrase, or node, or cluster, of words includes every essential element of the poem: its consonantal and assonantal sound-colour, style of vocabulary, and pace; as one cell can contain the information necessary to grow a complete organism. I am also inclined to think that if I were able to follow every possible clue, it would reveal itself as containing the poem's entire potential subject matter encoded in those few words – though here I am on less firm ground. It is '– a little thing, the size of a hazelnut . . .', which has to be investigated with extreme care and delicacy. Letting the poem emerge and reveal itself is like being witness to a process of crystallisation, because the form is implicit in its content, the content enclosed in its form.

Poems are dances. I think of Siva and his dance of creation and destruction and re-creation, the dance of the atoms, angels dancing on the head of a pin (which signifies the multitude of meanings and associations co-existing in perhaps only one word – but only because that word is placed exactly where it is in relation to every other word around it, which are also angels dancing), the Hasidic dance of praise and celebration. Poem and dance are the most primitive and most enduring expressions of the sense and joy of being alive.

This is how a poem begins, and if I am lucky, after a certain amount of time I will be left with enough material to give a reasonable hope of finishing it. But a poem can only be worked on for so long, as dough should only be kneaded for a certain time, then covered and put aside to rise. There must be a period of incubation. The next stages involve other aspects of the mind: knowledge, memory, intelligence, and self-criticism, the components of poetic skill (one of the most important being knowing when to stop). As Wallace Stevens wrote, 'The poet represents the mind in the act of defending us against itself.'

Being a poet can be a cause of suffering, yet it brings the greatest excitement and pleasure I know. In his introduction to John Clare's poems, James Reeves says, 'The writing of a fully expressive poem, whatever the theme, can only bring the true poet happiness. Happiness and suffering have their origin in the same cause – an excess of feeling, sudden or gradual, brief or long-lasting. The dividing line is soon crossed. The poet's abnormal sensibility makes him a pioneer in feeling, painful or pleasant; the value of poetry lies in the discovery of new emotion.' Although the expression of suffering is a way to free oneself from it, poetry is not the inevitable product of the unavoidable suffering which is every thinking being's lot. But as Baudelaire wrote in his study of Poe, the poet cannot freely determine his condition – Providence has 'prepared him for it from the cradle', 'dedicated him to the altar', 'consecrated him, so to speak'. The poet's only freedom is 'transforming this curse into a blessing . . . for poetry is liberation within this destiny, and the being who avoids this one avenue of escape is simply crushed; there will be no other way out'. Perhaps the flaying of Marsyas by Apollo, leader of the Muses and inspirer of sibyls and poets (from whom not even the Muse of Poetry can grant protection) is a metaphor for the special suffering of the poet, who in spite of the most glorious effort can never hope to win his or her challenge to the god.

RUTH FAINLIGHT

## Introspection of a Sibyl

If only I could be aware of what is happening
in that void, that gap, that murky, fathomless cleft
where space and time must exist
between inspiration and the sound of my own voice:
the truth I never once have heard
a moment earlier than my listeners.

But I am no more conscious of the prophecies
than I can understand the language of birds.
A bird is singing now.
In spite of legend, like everyone else,
I wonder and guess at its message.
My oracles come like bird-song – or how I imagine
they must begin to sing – by instinct:
neither needing nor able to think.

The most terrible phrases burst from my mouth.
My profession is to doom strangers.
Already, as a girl,
playing ball with my friends in the village square
or feeding my tame pigeon, I remember
being even more appalled than my parents
by what I'd say: an unforgivable insult
dealt out in all innocence, or a blurted sentence
like a gift to confirm good fortune.

How I admire control, and yearn to achieve it.
I've become almost grateful to those who control me.
Before, I never knew when it would begin,
the demon or angel invade me;
realised by the closed, startled expressions
on the faces of those standing round
– as though shutters crashed down –
that again I'd defined or foretold,
unerringly exposed the poor secret
some old man kept hidden all his life:

with sight as sharp as an eagle
who spots the single darting creature
veering back and forth, exhausted,
on a barren rocky mountainside,
maddened by the shadow of its wings –
and heavier than every element,
surer than the laws of gravity,
swoops for the kill.

After a few times, you recognise
a universal wariness. It takes longer
to fear yourself, to accept the certainty
of never illuminating that blankness –
that vital hiatus when the demon or angel,
the god, perhaps, takes possession
and you don't exist
yet have the power of a god.

Panic of falling – said to be
the sole inborn fear of a human infant.
Deeper than fear, I've learned, lies the greatest pleasure:
nausea and exhilaration of plummetting free –
the glee of surrender of nullity,
temptation more primal than any craving
for security: watching
the slow retreat of the gods, their stronghold
in flames, withdrawing from toppling towers,
abandoning our earth forever.

And the price for such knowledge? To have
absolutely no command over your life,
your words – no possibility
of calculated effects or tactics or policy.
But how useful you can be to others; and how lucky
if rather than burning or stoning, they protect you,
feed you, and let the simple folk praise you,
keep you safe as a caged bird –
and call you a sibyl.

## The Other

Whatever I find if I search will be wrong.
I must wait: sternest trial of all, to contain myself,
Sit passive, receptive, and patient, empty
Of every demand and desire, until
That other, that being I never would have found
Though I spent my whole life in the quest, will step
Clear of the shadows, approach like a wild, awkward child.

And this will be the longest task: to attend,
To open myself. To still my energy
Is harder than to use it in any cause.
Yet surely she will only be revealed
By pushing against the grain of my ardent nature
That always yearns for choice. I feel it painful
And strong as a birth in which there is no pause.

I must hold myself back from every lure of action
To let her come closer, a wary smile on her face,
One arm lifted: to greet me or ward off attack –
I cannot decipher that uncertain gesture.
I must even control the pace of my breath
Until she has drawn her circle near enough
To capture the note of her faint reedy voice.

And then as in dreams, when a language unspoken
Since times before childhood is recalled (when
I was as timid as she, my forgotten sister –
Her presence my completion and reward), I begin
To understand, in fragments, the message she waited
So long to deliver. Loving her I shall learn
My own secret at last from the words of her song.

## Anticipated

This month I've watched the moon through every change
from thinnest crescent into ripeness, from August
langour into clear September. Unseen
between two darknesses, full moon will be

tomorrow morning, just before noon. Tomorrow
night, hours after the unmarked climax,
her strength already waning, will be too late.
Tonight her energies are at their height.

Full moon used to awe me, craze me — now
I feel equal to her power. This
moment perhaps I too have reached an acme,
and the over-arching sky, the garden trees
with their rustlings and shadows, their nightingale-language,
are satellites circling around the centre
everything on earth anticipates
and this one night allows me to become.

## Stubborn

My Stone-Age self still scorns
attempts to prove us more
than upright animals
whose powerful skeletons
and sinewy muscled limbs
were made to be exhausted
by decades of labour
not subdued by thought,

despises still those dreamers
who forget, poets
who ignore, heroes
who defy mortality
while risking every failure,
spirits unsatisfied
by merely their own
bodily survival.

I know her awful strength.
I know how panic, envy,
self-defence, are mixed
with her tormented rage
because they will deny
her argument that nothing

but the body's pleasure,
use, and comfort, matters.

Guarding her cave and fire
and implements, stubborn
in her ignorance,
deaf to all refutation,
I know she must insist
until the hour of death
she cannot feel the pain
that shapes and haunts me.

## The Prism

Braided like those plaits of multi-
coloured threads my mother kept
in her workbox (beige, flesh, and fawn
for mending stockings, primary tones
to match our playclothes, grey and black
for Daddy's business suits), or Medusa-
coils of telephone wires, vivid
as internal organs exposed in their packed
logic under the pavement, nestling
in the gritty London clay,
associations fray into messages:

codes to unravel, cords to follow
out of prison, poems which make
no concession, but magnify
the truth of every note and colour,
indifferent whether they blind or deafen
or ravish or are ignored; the blueprint
of a shelter against the glare
– and the waterfall to build it near –
the perfect place to sit and hear
that choir of hymning voices, and watch
the prism of the rainbow spray.

## Here

*Feels that there is no
space that she can call
her own
she's continually put
into groups*

Here, like a rebel queen
exiled to the borderlands,
the only role I can assume
is Patience, the only gesture,
to fold my hands and smooth
my robe, to be the seemly one,

the only precept, always
to know the truth, even if forced
to silence, never to deny
my unrepentant nature.
I am my own tamer.
This life is the instrument.

And yet the iron hand wears
such a velvet glove,
and dreams and memories
of prelapsarian happiness –
simple actions which, when
first performed, lacked that content –

return to slow my steps
as I climb up and down between
the parlour and the kitchen
to fill my watering-can again
and give the plants their ration,
makes me question that self-image.

Some power, created by
an altered vision, moving
to a different rhythm,
annihilates the past, revealing
space enough for another
universe. And there,

where needs and wishes synchronize,
where truth is changed and laws
revised, the capital has fallen
to a friendly tribe,
and I can leave this exile
when I choose, or rule from here.

# Definition

Who told me my place?
It takes generations
To breed such a true believer –
I am of the race
Of dutiful captives; it needed
Centuries, millenia, to produce
Someone who instinctively knew
The only movement possible
Was up or down:
Spurting ascent to heaven's
Pleasures and mysteries, or else:
Madness, disgrace, chaotic
Infernal glee.
No space for me on the earth's surface.
Horizontal equates with delusive
When only the vertical
Remains open to my use
And influence.
But I am released by language,
I escape through speech:
Which has no dimensions,
Demands no local habitation
Or allegiance, which sets me free
From whomsoever's definition:
Jew, poet, woman.


# It Must

Friends, sisters, are you used to your face in the mirror?
Can you accept or even recognise it?
Don't be angry, answer me frankly, excuse
the question's crudity. I can't – no matter
how often I take the little square of glass
from my bag, or furtively glance into shop-windows,
the face reflected back is always a shock.

Those scars and wrinkles, the clumping of pigment
into moles, spots, faulty warty growths
around hairline and neck, the way skin's texture changes
absolutely, becomes roughened and scaly,
coarse-grained, every pore visible, as though
the magnification were intensified: horrible.
These days, I prefer firmer flesh in close-up.

Younger, I remember how I stared, with a mixture
of attraction, repulsion, and pity, at the cheeks of older
women – the sort I chose for friends. Did they
need me as much as I idealized them?
There seemed something splendid and brave about such raddled
features, crusted and blurred with the same heavy make-up
I've taken to wearing – warpaint, if, as they say,
the real function of warpaint is to bolster
the uncertain warrior's spirit, more than to
undermine and terrify his opponent.

Now, I long to ask my friends these very
questions and compare reactions, blurt out
the taboo words. But we're so polite, so lavish
with compliments, tender, protective – cherishing
the common hurt: tenderness of bruised flesh,
darkness under the eyes from held-back tears,
watery blisters on frost-touched fruit already
decaying, marked by death's irregularities.

Friends, tell me the truth. Do you also
sometimes feel a sudden jaunty indifference,
or even better, extraordinary moments
when you positively welcome the new
face that greets you from the mirror like
a mother – not your own mother, but that other
dream-figure of she-you-always-yearned-for.
Your face, if you try, can become hers. It must.

## Gloria

However she's personified
Or represented,
I won't forget
How space expands inside me,
Can easily contain
A million goddesses or concepts.

Sophia, Anima, or Kali,
Black or white, death or wisdom,
The central fire
Or all-engulfing water:

My muse is in myself;
And as all past and future
Exist between my own two eyes,
My living need
Is symbolised
By her resplendent figure.

She makes me dance,
She frightens me at night
With horrors,
Leads me to the burning-place.

She stands behind the mountains
Like the sun,
And lifts her arms to show
That they are only flesh,
That all this valley is alive
Because she wills it so.

## Lilith

Lilith, Adam's first companion,
Assumed her equality.
For this she was banished.

God had created her
From the same earth as Adam.
She stood her ground, amazed
By the idea of differences.

Adam and God were embarrassed,
Humiliated. It was true –
They had been formed
At the same time, the two
Halves of His reflection.

Her expectations
Should have seemed justified.
But Adam needed to understand God.
A creature must now worship him,
Constrained and resentful
As he was. God encouraged him.

To guard His mystery, God
Caused Adam to swoon. There, when he awoke,
Awaited Eve, the chattel.

Eyes downcast, his phallus
The first thing she noticed.
The snake reminded her of it.
Easy to equate the two.

That nagging ache in his side
Where the rib was extracted
(In memory of which
The soldier thrust his spear)
Keeps Adam irritable.

Lilith's disgrace thus defined
Good and evil. She would be
Outside, the feared, the alien,
Hungry and dangerous.
His seed and Eve's fruit
At hazard from her rage.

Good wives make amulets
Against her, to protect themselves.
Lilith is jealous.

## The Future

The future is timid and wayward
and wants to be courted, will not
respond to threats or coaxing,
and hears excuses only
when she feels secure.

Doubt, uproar, jeers,
vengeful faces roughened
by angry tears, the harsh
odours of self-importance,
are what alarm her most.

Nothing you do will lure her
from the corner where
she waits like a nun of a closed
order or a gifted young
dancer, altogether

the creature of her vocation,
with those limits and strengths.
Trying to reassure her,
find new alibis
and organise the proof

of your enthralment and
devotion, seems totally useless –
though it teaches how
to calm your spirit, move
beyond the problem's overt

cause and one solution –
until the future, soothed now,
starts to plot another
outcome to the story:
your difficult reward.

# SYLVIA PLATH

**Sylvia Plath** was born in 1932 in Massachusetts, where she grew up. She was the daughter of a German mother, and an Austrian father who died when she was six.

Plath discovered her taste and talent for writing very young, and by 16 was behaving like a professional writer, researching markets and sending out manuscripts. She did well at school and won a scholarship to the prestigious Smith's women's college. There she won a scholarship to study English at Newnham College, Cambridge. In England she met and married the poet Ted Hughes.

After her first book of poems, *The Colossus*, was published by Heinemann in 1960, she wrote a novel, three more books of poems, and some stories. The novel, *The Bell Jar*, was published under a pseudonym in 1963, shortly before she committed suicide. The three collections were published posthumously: *Ariel* in 1965, and *Winter Trees* and *Crossing the Water* in 1971. In 1981 Faber published her *Collected Poems*. Also available are her *Letters Home* (1976), edited by her mother Aurelia Schober Plath, and a prose selection, *Johnny Panic and the Bible of Dreams* (1977).

ABOVE: *Sylvia Plath with her children and mother in Devon, July 1962.*

# Sylvia Plath by JENI COUZYN

On February 11th, 1963, at the age of thirty, Sylvia Plath secured her two children in their room with the window open, then sealed herself in the kitchen and inhaled gas till she was dead.

Many male reviewers, in the twenty years since her suicide, have tried to explain her death by tracing it back as a neurotic death-wish, visible from her earliest poems.

Like all poets, Plath *was* attentive to death. Death gives life its cutting edge, its meaning, its light and shadow. For the poet, death is the essential white on the palette – no colour can be mixed true without containing it. Plath's attempted suicide while at university (a relatively common occurrence amongst sensitive students under pressure) gave her access to the precious knowledge of death from an early age.

Plath was not neurotic and black in her temperament. On the contrary, she believed her life was in some sense charmed – that good fortune was her closest friend, and that, with dedication and hard work, she would always achieve the best possible with her life. The rage and despair in the poems for which she is famous reflect rather an intolerably painful shattering of her high expectations of joy and success.

Women reviewers, on the other hand, have concentrated on the fact that her marriage bound her into a frustrating domestic role while her husband took over the role of successful poet.

Marriage is often a central issue in studies of women writers, and this is particularly true in the case of Plath. She was a poet with an excellent mind, but her expectations for her emotional life came straight from glossy magazines. A woman had to be beautiful, brilliant, and feminine to attract her man. Her man had to be big and strong and handsome, brilliant and kind. They would fall passionately in love, and get married, and have children, and this was the gateway to true happiness.

Her man turned out to be the poet Ted Hughes, who fitted the heroic image exactly, and Plath set about adoring him with the extremity of passion characteristic of her. The couple were married four months after their first meeting, while Plath was still reading for her Cambridge degree.

The catch to the story of true happiness for Plath was the "feminine" clause (as it is for all women who believe in it). No sooner had she fallen in love with Hughes, than she was writing to her mother in America with an urgent request for her *Joy of Cooking* – 'It's the one book I really miss!' In the first year of her marriage she wrote to her mother: 'I should not have three jobs – writing, cooking and housekeeping, and studying for tough exams.' (Not included in this formidable list is typing and sending out manuscripts for both Hughes and herself – no less than twenty out at any one time.) She goes on in the same letter with naivete that would be comical if it weren't so sadly prophetic: 'We don't want children for at least several years yet. Until we're well off enough financially to afford a housekeeper . . . so I won't be torn between domestic chores and my writing fulfillment, which is my deepest health.'

The housekeeper, of course, never materialised, but the babies did, and Plath discovered that babies do not combine with poetry. For the first happy years of their marriage, Hughes's and Plath's careers had both been going well, running on a roughly parallel course. But the with the arrival of Frieda, their first baby, they swerved in opposite directions. Hughes rose to success and fame with dazzling speed, Plath plummetted into obscurity and despair almost as fast.

The London literary establishment was, and still is, a tight Oxbridge-dominated network of men. Plath naively believed that this bias would make it easier for a talented Cambridge woman to succeed (especially if she were attractive as well). Typical of women brainwashed in a sexist society, she saw other women as competition, but men as an exciting challenge. She courted them, respected them, flattered them, and believed they would treat her with justice.

Consequently, when her first book, *The Colossus*, was published and faintly praised with sparse, patronising reviews, she felt it as a deep personal failure. She tended to measure her success by how much money she earned from her work, and was bitterly disappointed by her book's reception: 'Since I got no prize or any American publisher, they [Heinemann] haven't bothered to advertise it, so I probably won't make a penny on it unless I get some award later to call it to the public's attention.'

In the seven months following Frieda's birth in April 1960, Plath's letters show mounting frustration about her own lack of time and concentration to work. But from the time of the publication of *The Colossus* in October, her frustration hardened into depression and anger.

During that year, Plath wrote only a dozen poems, and herself wrote of them in her poem 'Stillborn': 'These poems do not live: it's a sad diagnosis'. She responded to the arrival of her babies with excitement and delight, and at first was optimistic that she would soon tuck housework and babies into a routine that allowed her freedom to return to work almost immediately. But as it became clear that this plan was a fantasy, her despair and grief at not being able to write plunged her into crisis. The destruction of that part of herself she recognised as her 'deepest health' became an agony that must have made her difficult to live with, impossible to love. It's hard to imagine, for example, feeling tender towards a wife as angry as Plath in 'Zoo Keeper's Wife', or as depressed as in 'A Life'.

Hughes, on the other hand, was working prolifically, and receiving acclaim for everything he did. Within six weeks of Frieda's birth, he had arranged to work at a friend's study away from home. Driven by the powerful wind of his own genius, he chose to follow it. Plath herself seems to have accepted this as the inevitable course for him. She wrote to her mother: 'It's impossible for him to work in this little place with me cleaning and caring for the baby . . . I find my first concern is that Ted has peace and quiet.'

When Plath herself was once asked if writing poetry was a source of satisfaction for her, her answer was: 'Oh satisfaction! I don't think I could live without it. It's like water or bread, or something absolutely essential to me.' In the rapture before her marriage, she had written of Hughes: 'Ted says he never read poems by a woman like mine; they are strong and full and rich – not quailing and whining like Teasdale or simple lyrics like Millay . . .' In the literary world they inhabited, women poets were not taken seriously, and when her work dried up with the arrival of her babies, no one appears to have recognised the source of her anguish.

Peace and quiet for Hughes meant retreat not only from domestic duties, but from the spiritual chaos Plath had plunged into when she stopped working. However, between the collapse of their marriage in June 1962, and her death in February 1963, Plath wrote sixty poems – most of her major work. Although she was writing from a state of intolerable emotional pain, her genius was released in an unstoppable flow that continued until a few days before her death.

*From* **A Comparison**

How I envy the novelist!

I imagine him – better say her, for it is the women I look to for a parallel – I imagine her, then, pruning a rosebush with a large pair of shears, adjusting her spectacles, shuffling about among the teacups, humming, arranging ashtrays or babies, absorbing a slant of light, a fresh edge to the weather and piercing, with a kind of modest, beautiful X-ray vision, the psychic interiors of her neighbors – her neighbors on trains, in the dentist's waiting room, in the corner teashop. To her, this fortunate one, what is there that *isn't* relevant! Old shoes can be used, doorknobs, airletters, flannel nightgowns, cathedrals, nail varnish, jet planes, rose arbors and budgerigars; little mannerisms – the sucking at a tooth, the tugging at a hemline – any weird or warty or fine or despicable thing. Not to mention emotions, motivations – those rumbling, thunderous shapes. Her business is Time, the way it shoots forward, shunts back, blooms, decays and double exposes itself. Her business is people in Time. And she, it seems to me, has all the time in the world. She can take a century if she likes, a generation, a whole summer.

I can take about a minute.

I'm not talking about epic poems. We all know how long *they* can take. I'm talking about the smallish, unofficial garden-variety poem. How shall I describe it? – a door opens, a door shuts. In between you have had a glimpse: a garden, a person, a rainstorm, a dragonfly, a heart, a city. I think of those round glass Victorian paperweights which I remember, yet can never find – a far cry from the plastic mass-productions which stud the toy counters in Woolworths. This sort of paperweight is a clear globe, self-complete, very pure, with a forest or village or family group within it. You turn it upside down, then back. It snows. Everything is changed in a minute. It will never be the same in there – not the fir trees, nor the gables, nor the faces.

So a poem takes place.

And there is really so little room! So little time! The poet becomes an expert packer of suitcases:

> The apparition of these faces in the crowd;
> Petals on a wet black bough.

There it is: the beginning and the end in one breath. How would the novelist manage that? In a paragraph? In a page? Mixing it, perhaps, like paint, with a little water, thinning it, spreading it out.

Now I am being smug, I am finding advantages.

[*c.* 1961]

## *From* Ocean 1212-W

My childhood landscape was not land but the end of the land – the cold, salt, running hills of the Atlantic. I sometimes think my vision of the sea is the clearest thing I own. I pick it up, exile that I am, like the purple 'lucky stones' I used to collect with a white ring all the way round, or the shell of a blue mussel with its rainbowy angel's finger-nail interior; and in one wash of memory the colors deepen and gleam, the early world draws breath.

Breath, that is the first thing. Something is breathing. My own breath? The breath of my mother? No, something else, something larger, farther, more serious, more weary. So behind shut lids I float awhile; – I'm a small sea captain, tasting the day's weather – battering rams at the seawall, a spray of grapeshot on my mother's brave geraniums, or the lulling shoosh-shoosh of a full, mirrory pool; the pool turns the quartz grits at its rim idly and kindly, a lady brooding at jewellery. There might be a hiss of rain on the pane, there might be wind sighing and trying the creaks of the house like keys. I was not deceived by these. The motherly pulse of the sea made a mock of such counterfeits. Like a deep woman, it hid a good deal; it had many faces, many delicate, terrible veils. It spoke of miracles and distances; if it could court, it could also kill. When I was learning to creep, my mother set me down on the beach to see what I thought of it. I crawled straight for the coming wave and was just through the wall of green when she caught my heels.

I often wonder what would have happened if I had managed to pierce that looking-glass. Would my infant gills have taken over, the salt in my blood? For a time I believed not in God nor Santa Claus, but in mermaids. They seemed as logical and possible to me as the brittle twig of a seahorse in the Zoo aquarium or the skates lugged up on the lines of cursing Sunday fishermen – skates the shape of old pillowslips with the full, coy lips of women.

And I recall my mother, a sea-girl herself, reading to me and my brother – who came later – from Matthew Arnold's 'Forsaken Merman':

Sand-strewn caverns, cool and deep,
Where the winds are all asleep;
Where the spent lights quiver and gleam;
Where the salt weed sways in the stream;
Where the sea-beasts rang'd all round
Feed in the ooze of their pasture-ground;
Where the sea-snakes coil and twine

Dry their mail and bask in the brine;
Where great whales come sailing by,
Sail and sail with unshut eye,
Round the world for ever and aye.

I saw the gooseflesh on my skin. I did not know what made it. I was not cold. Had a ghost passed over? No, it was the poetry. A spark flew off Arnold and shook me, like a chill. I wanted to cry; I felt very odd. I had fallen into a new way of being happy.

. . . . .

Hot April. I warmed my bottom on the mica-bright stone of my grandmother's steps, staring at the stucco wall, with its magpie design of eggstones, fan shells, colored glass. My mother was in hospital. She had been gone three weeks. I sulked. I would do nothing. Her desertion punched a smouldering hole in my sky. How could she, so loving and faithful, so easily leave me? My grandmother hummed and thumped out her bread dough with sup-pressed excitement. Viennese, Victorian, she pursed her lips, she would tell me nothing. Finally she melted a little. I would have a surprise when mother came back. It would be something nice. It would be – a baby.

A baby.

I hated babies. I who for two and a half years had been the centre of a tender universe felt the axis wrench and a polar chill immobilize my bones. I would be a bystander, a museum mammoth. Babies!

Even my grandfather, on the glassed-in verandah, couldn't woo me from my huge gloom. I refused to hide his pipe in the rubber plant and make it a pipe tree. He stalked off in his sneakers, wounded too, but whistling. I waited till his shape rounded Water Tower Hill and dwindled in the direction of the sea promenade; its ice-cream and hotdog stalls were boarded up still, in spite of the mild pre-season weather. His lyrical whistle beckoned me to adventure and forget-ting. But I didn't want to forget. Hugging my grudge, ugly and prickly, a sad sea urchin, I trudged off on my own, in the opposite direction toward the forbidding prison. As from a star I saw, coldly and soberly, the *separateness* of everything. I felt the wall of my skin: I am I. That stone is a stone. My beautiful fusion with the things of this world was over.

The tide ebbed, sucked back into itself. There I was, a reject, with the dried black seaweed whose hard beads I liked to pop, hollowed orange and grapefruit halves and a garbage of shells. All at once, old and lonely, I eyed these – razor clams, fairy boats, weedy mussels, the oyster's pocked grey lace (there was never a pearl) and tiny white

'ice-cream cones'. You could always tell where the best shells were –
at the rim of the last wave, marked by a mascara of tar. I picked up,
frigidly, a stiff pink starfish. It lay at the heart of my palm, a joke
dummy of my own hand. Sometimes I nursed starfish alive in jam
jars of seawater and watched them grow back lost arms. On this day,
this awful birthday of otherness, my rival, somebody else, I flung the
starfish against a stone. Let it perish. It had no wit.

I stubbed my toe on the round, blind stones. They paid no notice.
They didn't care. I supposed they were happy. The sea waltzed off
into nothing, into the sky – the dividing line on this calm day almost
invisible. I knew, from school, the sea cupped the bulge of the world
like a blue coat, but my knowledge somehow never connected with
what I *saw* – water drawn half-way up the air, a flat, glassy blind;
the snail trails of steamers along the rim. For all I could tell, they
circled that line forever. What lay behind it? 'Spain,' said owl-eyed
Harry Bean, my friend. But the parochial map of my mind couldn't
take it in. Spain. Mantillas and gold castles and bulls. Mermaids on
rocks, chests of jewels, the fantastical. A piece of which the sea,
ceaselessly eating and churning, might any minute beach at my feet.
As a sign.

A sign of what?

A sign of election and specialness. A sign I was not forever to be
cast out. And I *did* see a sign. Out of a pulp of kelp, still shining, with
a wet, fresh smell, reached a small, brown hand. What would it be?
What did I *want* it to be? A mermaid, a Spanish infanta?

What it was, was a monkey.

Not a real monkey, but a monkey of wood. Heavy with the water
it had swallowed and scarred with tar, it crouched on its pedestal,
remote and holy, long-muzzled and oddly foreign. I brushed it and
dried it and admired its delicately carved hair. It looked like no
monkey I had ever seen eating peanuts and moony-foolish. It had the
noble pose of a simian Thinker. I realize now that the totem I so
lovingly undid from its caul of kelp (and have since, alas, mislaid
with the other baggage of childhood) was a Sacred Baboon.

So the sea, perceiving my need, had conferred a blessing.

. . . . .

My final memory of the sea is of violence – a still, unhealthily yellow
day in 1939, the sea molten, steely-slick, heaving at its leash like a
broody animal, evil violets in its eye. Anxious telephone calls crossed
from my grandmother, on the exposed oceanside, to my mother, on
the bay. My brother and I, kneehigh still, imbibed the talk of tidal
waves, high ground, boarded windows and floating boats like a

miracle elixir. The hurricane was due at nightfall. In those days, hurricanes did not bud in Florida and bloom over Cape Cod each autumn as they now do – bang, bang, bang, frequent as firecrackers on the Fourth and whimsically named after women. This was a monstrous speciality, a leviathan. Our world might be eaten, blown to bits. We wanted to be in on it.

The sulphurous afternoon went black unnaturally early, as if what was to come could not be star-lit, torch-lit, looked at. The rain set in, one huge Noah douche. Then the wind. The world had become a drum. Beaten, it shrieked and shook. Pale and elated in our beds, my brother and I sipped our nightly hot drink. We would, of course, not sleep. We crept to a blind and hefted it a notch. On a mirror of rivery black our faces wavered like moths, trying to pry their way in. Nothing could be seen. The only sound was a howl, jazzed up by the bangs, slams, groans and splinterings of objects tossed like crockery in a giant's quarrel. The house rocked on its root. It rocked and rocked and rocked its two small watchers to sleep.

The wreckage the next day was all one could wish – overthrown trees and telephone poles, shoddy summer cottages bobbing out by the lighthouse and a litter of the ribs of little ships. My grand-mother's house had lasted, valiant – though the waves broke right over the road and into the bay. My grandfather's seawall had saved it, neighbors said. Sand buried her furnace in golden whorls; salt stained the upholstered sofa and a dead shark filled what had been the geranium bed, but my grandmother had her broom out, it would soon be right.

And this is how it stiffens, my vision of that seaside childhood. My father died, we moved inland. Whereon those nine first years of my life sealed themselves off like a ship in a bottle – beautiful, inacces-sible, obsolete, a fine, white flying myth.

[c. 1961]

SYLVIA PLATH

## Zoo Keeper's Wife

I can stay awake all night, if need be—
Cold as an eel, without eyelids.
Like a dead lake the dark envelops me,
Blueblack, a spectacular plum fruit.
No airbubbles start from my heart, I am lungless
And ugly, my belly a silk stocking
Where the heads and tails of my sisters decompose.
Look, they are melting like coins in the powerful juices—

The spidery jaws, the spine bones bared for a moment
Like the white lines on a blueprint.
Should I stir, I think this pink and purple plastic
Guts bag would clack like a child's rattle,
Old grievances jostling each other, so many loose teeth.
But what do you know about that
My fat pork, my marrowy sweetheart, face-to-the-wall?
Some things of this world are indigestible.

You wooed me with the wolf-headed fruit bats
Hanging from their scorched hooks in the moist
Fug of the Small Mammal House.
The armadillo dozed in his sandbin
Obscene and bald as a pig, the white mice
Multiplied to infinity like angels on a pinhead
Out of sheer boredom. Tangled in the sweat-wet sheets
I remember the bloodied chicks and the quartered rabbits.

You checked the diet charts and took me to play
With the boa constrictor in the Fellows' Garden.
I pretended I was the Tree of Knowledge.
I entered your bible, I boarded your ark
With the sacred baboon in his wig and wax ears
And the bear-furred, bird-eating spider
Clambering round its glass box like an eight-fingered hand.
I can't get it out of my mind

How our courtship lit the tindery cages —
Your two-horned rhinoceros opened a mouth
Dirty as a bootsole and big as a hospital sink
For my cube of sugar: its bog breath

*Very direct
+ wbrupt - straint
+ no
point.*

Gloved my arm to the elbow.
The snails blew kisses like black apples.
Nightly now I flog apes owls bears sheep
Over their iron stile. And still don't sleep.


## Event


How the elements solidify!—
The moonlight, that chalk cliff
In whose rift we lie

Back to back. I hear an owl cry
From its cold indigo.
Intolerable vowels enter my heart.

The child in the white crib revolves and sighs,
Opens its mouth now, demanding.
His little face is carved in pained, red wood.

Then there are the stars—ineradicable, hard.
One touch: it burns and sickens.
I cannot see your eyes.

Where apple bloom ices the night
I walk in a ring,
A groove of old faults, deep and bitter.

Love cannot come here.
A black gap discloses itself.
On the opposite lip

A small white soul is waving, a small white maggot.
My limbs, also, have left me.
Who has dismembered us?

The dark is melting. We touch like cripples.

## Ariel

Stasis in darkness.
Then the substanceless blue
Pour of tor and distances.

God's lioness,
How one we grow,
Pivot of heels and knees!—The furrow

Splits and passes, sister to
The brown arc
Of the neck I cannot catch,

Nigger-eye
Berries cast dark
Hooks—

Black sweet blood mouthfuls,
Shadows.
Something else

Hauls me through air—
Thighs, hair;
Flakes from my heels.

White
Godiva, I unpeel—
Dead hands, dead stringencies.

And now I
Foam to wheat, a glitter of seas.
The child's cry

Melts in the wall.
And I
Am the arrow,

The dew that flies
Suicidal, at one with the drive
Into the red

Eye, the cauldron of morning.

## Nick and the Candlestick

I am a miner. The light burns blue.
Waxy stalactites
Drip and thicken, tears

The earthen womb
Exudes from its dead boredom.
Black bat airs

Wrap me, raggy shawls,
Cold homicides.
They weld to me like plums.

Old cave of calcium
Icicles, old echoer.
Even the newts are white,

Those holy Joes.
And the fish, the fish—
Christ! they are panes of ice,

A vice of knives,
A piranha
Religion, drinking

Its first communion out of my live toes.
The candle
Gulps and recovers its small altitude,

Its yellows hearten.
O love, how did you get here?
O embryo

Remembering, even in sleep,
Your crossed position.
The blood blooms clean

In you, ruby.
The pain
You wake to is not yours.

Love, love,
I have hung our cave with roses,
With soft rugs—

The last of Victoriana.
Let the stars
Plummet to their dark address,

Let the mercuric
Atoms that cripple drip
Into the terrible well,

You are the one
Solid the spaces lean on, envious.
You are the baby in the barn.


**The Night Dances**

A smile fell in the grass.
Irretrievable!

And how will your night dances
Lose themselves. In mathematics?

Such pure leaps and spirals—
Surely they travel

The world forever, I shall not entirely
Sit emptied of beauties, the gift

Of your small breath, the drenched grass
Smell of your sleeps, lilies, lilies.

Their flesh bears no relation.
Cold folds of ego, the calla,

And the tiger, embellishing itself—
Spots, and a spread of hot petals.

The comets
Have such a space to cross,

Such coldness, forgetfulness.
So your gestures flake off—

Warm and human, then their pink light
Bleeding and peeling

Through the black amnesias of heaven.
Why am I given

These lamps, these planets
Falling like blessings, like flakes

Six-sided, white
On my eyes, my lips, my hair

Touching and melting.
Nowhere.


**Poppies in October**

Even the sun-clouds this morning cannot manage such skirts.
Nor the woman in the ambulance
Whose red heart blooms through her coat so astoundingly—

A gift, a love gift
Utterly unasked for
By a sky

Palely and flamily
Igniting its carbon monoxides, by eyes
Dulled to a halt under bowlers.

O my God, what am I
That these late mouths should cry open
In a forest of frost, in a dawn of cornflowers.

## Fever 103°

Pure? What does it mean?
The tongues of hell
Are dull, dull as the triple

Tongues of dull, fat Cerberus
Who wheezes at the gate. Incapable
Of licking clean

The aguey tendon, the sin, the sin.
The tinder cries.
The indelible smell

Of a snuffed candle!
Love, love, the low smokes roll
From me like Isadora's scarves, I'm in a fright

One scarf will catch and anchor in the wheel.
Such yellow sullen smokes
Make their own element. They will not rise,

But trundle round the globe
Choking the aged and the meek,
The weak

Hothouse baby in its crib,
The ghastly orchid
Hanging its hanging garden in the air,

Devilish leopard!
Radiation turned it white
And killed it in an hour.

Greasing the bodies of adulterers
Like Hiroshima ash and eating in.
The sin. The sin.

Darling, all night
I have been flickering, off, on, off, on.
The sheets grow heavy as a lecher's kiss.

Three days. Three nights.
Lemon water, chicken
Water, water make me retch.

I am too pure for you or anyone.
Your body
Hurts me as the world hurts God. I am a lantern—

My head a moon
Of Japanese paper, my gold beaten skin
Infinitely delicate and infinitely expensive.

Does not my heat astound you. And my light.
All by myself I am a huge camellia
Glowing and coming and going, flush on flush.

I think I am going up,
I think I may rise—
The beads of hot metal fly, and I, love, I

Am a pure acetylene
Virgin
Attended by roses,

By kisses, by cherubim,
By whatever these pink things mean.
Not you, nor him

Not him, nor him
(My selves dissolving, old whore petticoats)—
To Paradise.

 **The Applicant**


First, are you our sort of a person?
Do you wear
A glass eye, false teeth or a crutch,
A brace or a hook,
Rubber breasts or a rubber crotch,

Stitches to show something's missing? No, no? Then
How can we give you a thing?
Stop crying.
Open your hand.
Empty? Empty. Here is a hand

To fill it and willing
To bring teacups and roll away headaches
And do whatever you tell it.
Will you marry it?
It is guaranteed

To thumb shut your eyes at the end
And dissolve of sorrow.
We make new stock from the salt.
I notice you are stark naked.
How about this suit—

Black and stiff, but not a bad fit.
Will you marry it?
It is waterproof, shatterproof, proof
Against fire and bombs through the roof.
Believe me, they'll bury you in it.

Now your head, excuse me, is empty.
I have the ticket for that.
Come here, sweetie, out of the closet.
Well, what do you think of *that*?
Naked as paper to start

But in twenty-five years she'll be silver,
In fifty, gold.
A living doll, everywhere you look.
It can sew, it can cook,
It can talk, talk, talk.

It works, there is nothing wrong with it.
You have a hole, it's a poultice.
You have an eye, it's an image.
My boy, it's your last resort.
Will you marry it, marry it, marry it.

## Death & Co.

Two, of course there are two.
It seems perfectly natural now—
The one who never looks up, whose eyes are lidded
And balled, like Blake's,
Who exhibits

The birthmarks that are his trademark—
The scald scar of water,
The nude
Verdigris of the condor.
I am red meat. His beak

Claps sidewise: I am not his yet.
He tells me how badly I photograph.
He tells me how sweet
The babies look in their hospital
Icebox, a simple

Frill at the neck,
Then the flutings of their Ionian
Death-gowns,
Then two little feet.
He does not smile or smoke.

The other does that,
His hair long and plausive.
Bastard
Masturbating a glitter,
He wants to be loved.

I do not stir.
The frost makes a flower,
The dew makes a star,
The dead bell,
The dead bell.

Somebody's done for.

# Edge

The woman is perfected.
Her dead

Body wears the smile of accomplishment,
The illusion of a Greek necessity

Flows in the scrolls of her toga,
Her bare

Feet seem to be saying:
We have come so far, it is over.

Each dead child coiled, a white serpent,
One at each little

Pitcher of milk, now empty.
She has folded

Them back into her body as petals
Of a rose close when the garden

Stiffens and odours bleed
From the sweet, deep throats of the night flower.

The moon has nothing to be sad about,
Staring from her hood of bone.

She is used to this sort of thing.
Her blacks crackle and drag.

# JENNY JOSEPH

**Jenny Joseph** was born in 1932 in Birmingham. She read English at Oxford, where she was a scholar at St Hilda's. She has been a newspaper reporter, a pub landlady and a lecturer. Now a freelance writer and lecturer, she lives in London and Gloucestershire.

Her first book of poems, *The Unlooked-for Season* (Scorpion Press, 1960), won her a Gregory Award, and she won a Cholmondeley Award for her second collection, *Rose in the Afternoon* (Dent, 1974). Two further collections followed from Secker, *The Thinking Heart* (1978) and *Beyond Descartes* (1983). In 1985 her first work of fiction, *Persephone* – a novel-length story in poetry and prose – will appear from Bloodaxe. She has also published six children's books.

When I was 17 I heard the story about Lorca walking in the red light district of a town and recognising the words of a song a prostitute was singing. They were from a poem he had written. This at once for me became the ideal. It seemed the absolute of fame that what one wrote should be so much a part of the world as to rise to the lips of any Tom Dick or Harry, Joan Liz or Mary, unaware of authorship, like sayings, like the war songs, like ballads.

Ambitions change and over many years of trying to write and also to come to grips with ideas about art, my attitudes and my ability to express them have shifted. Now if I have an ambition it is a useless one for it is a "would have been" rather than something impossible that at least extracts some effort from you: now I would like to have been the person who created the doleful phrase "It's bein' so cheerful as keeps *me* goin'".

I was asked by some bright buttons of children the other day what made me into a poet. It would have been discourteous to say I didn't think of it like that, and discouraging to enquiring minds to suggest that your own version of your life is just one more story. I didn't want to sound self-pitying and say that if you can't jump over that dreadful pyramid of three piled benches in the gym class what can you do but take to books? I managed to say that I would rather describe myself as a writer, that I grew up in a household that liked books, but even more, words. People told me stories: jokes, anecdotes, puns, tricks, shaggy dog stories, discussion, justification, argument, explanations – everything that happened, or failed to happen – was turned into words.

I didn't think of it like this at the time of course and if I'd become a circus clown could no doubt find some causal traits in childhood. Perhaps it is something I have extracted to make the pattern that middle-age seems to wish to see in what has led up to it. Everyone, not only writers, makes up the "story of my life", but it is usually a story of the past. A writer out of habit draws the present into the story and, in so far as one writes out of the urgency of one's consciousness of "now", writing is personal. It comes out of, it makes, the story we are living.

The personal(ity) in the poem or story lasts, is fabricated for, that particular work, or series of works. Then another work, another "now", another story demands a different set-up. Even a prose discussion such as this is a frame-up. I delight in the variety of modes in English literature and enjoy listening to other languages to get a different verbal stance. I think attempts at translating, from one language to another, one form to another, are good training for a writer.

The current emphasis on poetry as "self-expression", "personal expression", "identity" I believe to be mistaken. There have been times when as a reader or spectator art has saved me because it takes off the heat of personal circumstances, cools the fiery matter along channels that lead into, and back from, the great wide sea of otherness. The cramping, inturned energy of the particular flows out into the general whose wider waves keep the personal (a top wobbling wildly under its own unstable force) from crashing. For a long time I thought eighteenth-century and Aristotelian dicta about poets being concerned with general truths and not 'numbering the streaks of the tulip' pedestrian and leading to stilted poetry. Now I begin to see what they meant:

> 'The business of the poet' said Imlac 'is to examine, not the individual but the species; to remark general properties and large appearances; he does not number the streaks of the tulip or describe the different shades in the verdure of the forest. He is to exhibit in his portraits of nature such prominent and striking features as recall the original to every mind . . .'

The continuation of this discussion (in Samuel Johnson's *Rasselas*) on all the things needed to become a poet is often left out:

> Imlac now felt the enthusiastic fit and was proceeding to aggrandize his own profession when the prince cried out: 'Enough! Thou hast convinced me that no human being can ever be a poet. Proceed with thy narration.'
>    'To be a poet' said Imlac 'is indeed very difficult.' 'So difficult' returned the prince 'that I will at present hear no more of his labours. Tell me whither you went when you had seen Persia.'

This generalizing, idealizing process starts with the very use of words. The word "table" must somewhere hold all tables, all aspects of table, all functions of table. Poetry, made of words, doubles the effect.

The mistaken emphasis springs from a confusion of two things: where art comes from and what it is. The first, which I too find fascinating, is of interest to anyone drawn by questions of how the human being functions. It is a natural-history interest, an interest in process. Piaget, who watched how and when children became what they are, most appropriately started by studying the size of one sort of snail relative to its position on the Swiss mountain it lived on. But the pearl *is* not the oyster, the grit, the wound. The flesh of our arm *is* not cabbage leaves, fibre of ox and water. How the Word can be made flesh is still one of the most mysterious paradoxes we can bear to entertain. As Rosemary Dinnage writing on Kafka suggests: 'All writers turn to words in order to solidify their apprehension of things, to fill some empty socket in the mind by gestures of evocation.' The connection between the subjective material of his diaries and letters and the 'marble objectivity' of his fiction is not a simple one, she says.

Other writers recognise Kafka's experience that once you put a thing into words you finish with it, you destroy it. Some writers will not discuss work coming up to boil in case talking "takes the steam out of it".

We get more frivolous as we get older – being so cheerful keeps us going – but the years I spent battling with ideas about art and trying to apply what I heard must have influenced my present attitudes, although these are shifting all the while. I went through other people, in so far as I understood what they were – or they through me – in order literally to understand, under-study, them. Emerging, I was again of course stuck with the limits that physique, temperament, training, tastes and circumstances impose, but with a change of emphasis, some enlargement. When I was 18 one of my concerns was that poetry should not be in a cul-de-sac off the highway of public interest, a gourmet's sauce to the meat. On the other hand I find the current self-conscious tailoring of the coat of art to what will have "popular" appeal both insulting and suffocating.

We have to accept that with our move away from tribalism everyone can choose some of the furniture of their mind so an artist is less and less sure that the references – and poetry depends more than other art on the resources of reference – will work. I think this was at the back of my use of the weather, seasons and daily circumstances in my writing. These still affected everyone. For me writing was an exploration of the world, not of the labyrinth of my own mind and presentation of unique treasures therefrom. I indulged in that in private conversation and letters. I used my own life only because it is material we have unique access to. I had not the knowledge, nor did I consider I had the right, to probe anybody else's quite so relentlessly. The use of dailiness got me dubbed as a "domestic" poet which I not only resent but disagree with. People who read a poem as a statement of information rather than a fabric of which the chosen tone is the warp often miss a double-take. They are unaware of the great variety of voices in our traditions of the use of English in literature. Writers cannot help but be mimics absorbing (most fruitfully when unconsciously) the verbal stances of the people they hear and read. Especially with poetry the choice of tone is part of the meaning, which accounts for its capacity to do two things at the same time. Robert Browning par excellence understood and used this. I have become more conscious of this in the last few years though my poetry exemplified it early on.

An artist can be – must be – an old person of the sea and yet present an apparent unity. Pieces of writing are different because they are in different forms.

I enjoy playing with rather involved schemes in short poems. The result may not be my best and perhaps my "theme" poems, which tend to be in paragraphs of blank verse, are the ones people think more important, but through my writing life I have written two sorts of poetry. There have been great works (often unwritten), schemes with a horrible tendency to grow too big for the room. And there have cropped up at irregular intervals apparently idle times when you gradually realise you are listening to something. If you can forget about being good or right you lose yourself once more, as when you were a child and knew poetry but had not heard of criticism, and you were excited with how beautiful – beautiful like the poetry you read – the words you put down were. It is one of the most impersonal things. It has nothing to do with self-expression or identity. It is an extension of the paltry self into the things that are interesting to learn and to be with – an escape into reality. The result of these spells of concentrating on what you are doing rather than worrying about the right thing, may be rubbish, especially if your taste is naturally bad, but something of that indulgence in your own taste, something of the secret enjoyment of treating yourself to your favourite piece of cake, should be there at some stage in writing if it is not to fall flat.

These are some of my thoughts on writing. I don't think they necessarily have much to do with the poems, for you write only what you can. The work of mine that comes nearest to writing what I wanted is *Persephone*. If we could be Chaucer, Emily Brontë, Beckett, Margaret Irwin et al we would be. Ideas about writing come from our desires, but our writing is what we are stuck with, as one is stuck with one's face. The poems are what we write when we have given up the difficult task of "being a poet" and, getting back to the story, tell our audience 'whither we went when we had seen Persia'.

JENNY JOSEPH

## Rose in the afternoon

Not rose of death:
Drawing in to your centre each wave of colour
That your arrested petals give to the air—
Dying inwardly the petals do not fall.

Nor rose of heaven:
Calm at the centre of this city
Monstrous moons, exuberance of stars
Have nothing to do with the light that you collect.
The light of the world has nourished your cut bloom
Drop by drop drawn down into your blood
As drop by drop your root took life from the ground.

Far down the river a cork popples the water
The motion quivers and rocks the air until
Rose in my room you catch and turn the movement
Mote by mote absorbed into your flesh
The vibrant morning tide within your veins.
Equally, hands moving in shuttered clubs
Though no light enters there to give time progress,
Flick flash-ringed fingers as red five black queen
Fall. Seeping through streets this gleam feeds you.

Day by day you calcify, embalming
The vigour you exhale. Fragile you have
Subdued the molten morning in your calyx
The palpitating golden fire that poured
Over the ridges of buildings, right angles, volutes;
And converted percussion of day to this calm strong flowing
Light lapping gentle round the afternoon;
Will equally subdue the night to come—
A ray shooting the dark – into a mere
Closure of a known twilight, not different state.

O rose in the afternoon, your only movement
The imperceptible falling in your blood,
Your vibrant stillness more speaking than all the voices,
If I could give you as answer, my sentence your statement
I would be dumb in peace with the light gone
And only your image waking in the dark.

## Dawn walkers

Anxious eyes loom down the damp-black streets
Pale staring girls who are walking away hard
From beds where love went wrong or died or turned away,
Treading their misery beneath another day
Stamping to work into another morning.

In all our youths there must have been some time
When the cold dark has stiffened up the wind
But suddenly, like a sail stiffening with wind,
Carried the vessel on, stretching the ropes, glad of it.

But listen to this now: this I saw one morning.
I saw a young man running, for a bus I thought,
Needing to catch it on this murky morning
Dodging the people crowding to work or shopping early.
And all heads stopped and turned to see how he ran
To see would he make it, the beautiful strong young man.
Then I noticed a girl running after, calling out 'John'.
He must have left his sandwiches I thought.
But she screamed 'John wait'. He heard her and ran faster,
Using his muscled legs and studded boots.
We knew she'd never reach him. 'Listen to me John.
Only once more' she cried. 'For the last time, John, please wait,
            please listen.'
He gained the corner in a spurt and she
Sobbing and hopping with her red hair loose
(Made way for by the respectful audience)
Followed on after, but not to catch him now.
Only that there was nothing left to do.

The street closed in and went on with its day.
A worn old man standing in the heat from the baker's
Said 'Surely to God the bastard could have waited'.

## Women at Streatham Hill

They stand like monuments or trees, not women,
Heavy and loaded on the common's edge
Pausing before the leaves' decline; far off
The railway runs through grass and bushes where
Slim girls and interested lovers seem
Another species, not just generation:
Butterflies flitting in the leaves, not stones.

    Nobody asks what they have done all day
    For who asks trees or stones what they have done?
    They root, they gather moss, they spread, they are.
    The busyness is in the birds about them.
    It would seem more removal than volition
    If once they were not there when men came home.

Ah giggling creamy beauties, can you think
*You* will withdraw into this private world
Weighted with shopping, spreading hands and feet,
Trunk gnarling, weatherworn? that if you get
All that your being hurls towards, like Daphne
Your sap will rise to nourish other things
Than suppliant arms and hair that glints and beckons?
Your bodies are keyed and spry, yet do you see
*Any*thing clearly through the grass-green haze
Hear anything but the murmur of desires?

    Bargains in bags, they separate towards home,
    Their talk a breeze that rustles topmost leaves
    Tickles the dust in crannies in the rock:
    Beetles that grind at roots it touches not.
    The women pull their thoughts in, easing like stones
    Where they are set, hiding the cavities.
    They care as little now to be disturbed
    As flighty daughters urgently want peace.

## Warning

When I am an old woman I shall wear purple
With a red hat which doesn't go, and doesn't suit me.
And I shall spend my pension on brandy and summer gloves
And satin sandals, and say we've no money for butter.
I shall sit down on the pavement when I'm tired
And gobble up samples in shops and press alarm bells
And run my stick along the public railings
And make up for the sobriety of my youth.
I shall go out in my slippers in the rain
And pick the flowers in other people's gardens
And learn to spit.

You can wear terrible shirts and grow more fat
And eat three pounds of sausages at a go
Or only bread and pickle for a week
And hoard pens and pencils and beermats and things in boxes.

But now we must have clothes that keep us dry
And pay our rent and not swear in the street
And set a good example for the children.
We must have friends to dinner and read the papers.

But maybe I ought to practise a little now?
So people who know me are not too shocked and surprised
When suddenly I am old, and start to wear purple.

## Another old tale

One small soldier going towards the mountain
'Ho, ho' shouting; 'I am not one to lurk
Waiting for the beast to kill me.
No; out and after it, trample its lair, push to its core.
That's my system.
Thus I am out from the last tight circle of corn
That shivers in the razed field, packed with fear
Great eyes between every stalk attracting death.
I am out and away before the beaters come,
Half-way to rifling their homestead.'

With flask, exercises, pemmy, courage up
Expert in preparation, custom-built equipment,
Off he goes, to fight Winter.
Through the storm he came, across the tundra
With never a tree, never a stake to support him.
The sun came out and sparkled on the snow.
'How right I was, see now' he breathed his song
And his own vapour on the air entranced him.
'The fight is to the brave. Come on. I prosper.'
He marched on, breathing rare air, using his substance.

Through the slow ages two white ears of glacier
Peered on the rim of the mountain six miles sheer
A bowl on the top of the sky,
Animal-intent, it paused, caught
By the tiny creeping movement across the plain
Drawing within its circle.

He used his food up in three days; in six
His skins were tattered; the everlasting rocks
Held thousands of years of ice packed in this present
And thousands yet to go.

Whistling, as he knew how, to let himself know
His lungs were in good shape, caring for his feet
He hardly had time to see where the sky's maelstrom
Opened and came down, the point where black and white
Meet in an extreme of blindness, itself blanked out
By the whirling *néant* exhaustless in its powering.

As of a vague white paw the abyss hit him
A cream-coloured tiger's cuff, absent-minded,
The pit of its eye swivelled on a far horizon.

The edge of a fly-wing mashed into the rock
Half-way down through this orb, has not less substance
Than this little speck of grit, propelled a half-inch
Dreaming a state called Summer, a world thought human.

## In memory of God

I suppose they would've shot the moon down,
If they could have, into little pieces,
To make a new one
Even while saying isn't it strange, isn't it beautiful.

Come, I will show you a marvel
Of man.

There on the green
A huge contraption in a palisade.
'You have here a perfect replica of a whale.
Every branch of knowledge known to man
(You name it, we got it) has gone into this project
To bring you the fabulous wonders of the deep.'

Yes, here's a panel
That tells you who gave grants for what to whom
And who the electrician was, and which boroughs
Raised a penny rate to send the team
To find the stuff to make the eyes – etcetera.
'Ask him not to touch, lady, would you mind? –
Just to look at, son, so you know what they looked like –
We need a grant for a pool, and another two thou to get it
Buoyant, so it would *move*. Then there's maintenance.'

Far in perpetual waters a creature turned
Coasted and turned in perfect machinations
Moving, like clouds at the edge of the world, untended
Simply itself in its extraordinary being:
Easy, so easy moving through the water.

Stupid men. All you had to do
To get a whale, was not to spend one penny, not do anything
But let be what miraculously was there.

No one on earth can make a whale again.
And when, because of what you have made way for
The rats over-run us, think of the mild wonders
We could have let keep the world:
Unclever, not like us, yet much more skilful
And useful, alas, in all their parts to man.

But being no use would probably not have saved you:
The strange shining disc that lights you to your extinction
Far over your dark pathways,
And even whatever caused the moon's pull, the life of waters
To maintain the whale –
They would put it in their pocket if they could.

## The inland sea

Did I tell you of a strange dream I had?
I was in the upper country, mule country,
The track twisting, dust, stone; sometimes,
Standing rare and beautiful, a thistle
On a cliff edge. White sky behind it.

Suddenly, singing
Was coming up the valley; and as it neared –
The little group, you could see that it travelled with them –
The green carpet of the valley floor:
Grasses and fronds with hanging heads, and mosses.

The fore man stood by me on the cliff
A Chinese ivory sage that fits in the palm
With every thousand hair in his beard distinct
And wrinkles lining a face as smooth as a pebble
But complete and whole; and this man spoke to me.

'It is the inland sea we seek,' he said
'And we will journey ever,' and round the mountain,
As they moved on like a shoal in the ravine bottom,
Winding as one, like a cloud across the sky,
Their distant singing swayed and ebbed with the wind
And I felt safe because these old men sought
The inland sea.

I remember a girl telling me
(Brown curly hair, fresh skin and open eyes
Sweet honest and innocent English abroad –
I don't think they are made like that any more –)
Of her meeting the man that she was now engaged to.

They had met and she dreamt that she was married to him
And the second time she saw him told him her dream.
She was not bold or fishing or plotting consequence
'Wasn't it strange' she'd said 'to have such a dream?'
And he asked her to marry him.

Why do I, a life time late, these years after
Talk of dreams, fabricating premises
When we both know it may be so or no
And not matter; when the direct truth
And the direct lie are mudded by convenience
And compromised;
When all is a game we would like to win, but know
The losing will shake us for only a little while
Before we slip back into our haze of self
Where all is slumber within wired-up walls?

Why? Listen. Come a little closer, near as you dare
To the edge of this spur. The soil's a little crumbly
But there are hawthorns, sloes and other bushes
Knitting the escarpment. Here is shade
And safety on the edge of danger. A place I found
By long trekking, retreating at times with care
Not to loosen rock, and going about
Another way until I found this nest.
Listen. Inch forward. What do you hear in the wind
That, freed from the bluffs, is meandering with the river?
Look up to the sky an instant, do you not see
Immense lakes of light lying within the clouds?
Part these grasses: spread out fair below
The hidden, ancient, still-fructifying source
Silent shines in sunlight.
Can you see? Come a bit nearer then. Now.
Look: we have come to the inland sea.

*From* **Persephone**
Two extracts


Those who turn their face to the wall
And cover their heads in blankets at midday
These are mine.
Those who smile and say 'Thank you, that would be nice' and never
          go,
These are mine.
Those who are found, when work has been agreed,
Paint got, gear kept, clothing bought and delivered
Who followed 'I'll be there for sure' with 'Don't fail me now'
And are found sitting in the yard, tools caked, old cans
Cluttered round inert ankles, socks with dead flies
Soaking in week-old wash-water;
Those who make a point
Of asking intently and urgently for help
And when one has struggled through rain to do so
Are nowhere, and the man who has struggled
Is later met with a righteous 'where were you then?'
These are mine.
Those who order all sorts of things through the post
To beautify their homes (to have a home)
And plan to make family trips (to make it a family)
And do not open the parcels and are asleep on Sundays,
Those who take the word for the deed, and sit listless in bars
Miles away from the scene they have suggested
Miles away from the one they suggested it to
Who now sits arranged, ready, and will sit so all evening,
These are mine.
And those who, not winning, stare behind glass
'My limbs not being moved for me, I cannot move them' –
Those who despair in the season for despair,
These, all these, are mine.


Come down with me
Whom I would call my followers
(But following suggests that you could move)
Come down,
You who turn from things,
Into my blank domain where the silence would suit you.

Here only worms and roots grow
Here's unstriving dust
Shells and scabs and the remains of things.
Only worms and roots, husks and cases
And even they
Are colourless and blind.

\* \* \*

You see this rain
Slanting out of a copper sky
Falling from the middle of the air
Not higher than the trees or buildings
Immense light still bright behind the edges
And the woman in a sunhat running out to save the washing,
And you hear it, how it soothes with its gentle patter
The crinkled earth:
Big soft drops you can separately hear, splashing;
A black rag flaps across the corner of the eye –
Blackbird homing from green –
And this rain is trickling down gulleys, into the splits
Of hard old tracks, stamped hard with sorrowing feet
Cracking with weariness and desiccation.
And if a seed, pushed by the winter wind
And rotted as a useless wisp of hay
Is licked into delight and rained upon
There stands your wheat.
Rain, you are loosening something in my bones
Soft fingers draw back coverings in my head.

Something undoes with a little lurch, rose
Of blood opening in the body
Body that pumps these rivers of the world –
Torrents of love to make the grass grow,
Persephone's moist breath in the rising corn.

*From* **Altarpiece**
Centrepiece: St Sebastian (Italian)

Faith struck Sebastian, got him
Hands twisted behind his back,

His heart thrust out
And other vulnerable parts he could not cover.

Now see Sebastian a prisoner there
The archer's patron by the archers hit
The soft white skin no day had looked upon
All parts exposed before the clothed crowd
Stretched for the tough little darts and the shafts of eyes
Armpits and groin tied open for their arrows.

The arrow of lust has hit him where it hurts
And he has no protection, for he looks
Upward into another element.
Died for the cause, for preaching love to men
Caught by the unconverted, no defence
And all his caring turned against him now.
Love tied his hands. He cannot catch the darts
Hurtling towards him and return them back.

It is not hand alone that shoots the shaft
Into the entrails of the body of love.
It was the word of Brutus, not the sword
Left Caesar undefended.
The word, like the barb on the shaft, feathers the dart
And fixes it in the skin against withdrawal.
They left him dead, relieved to have rooted out
The alien soldier from their body of men.

But love that stood him there thought otherwise.
Strange the seeping word, for lo at night
Sebastian carried to a little place
Where quiet and sure his wounds he struggles from
Helped by good women, fleshly life long done.
Set forth again by kindness on his voyage
Straightway to General Diocletian went
'Your servant, left for dead, reporting, Sir,
Ready for service, for see how little harmed
By arrows of the world my intent was.
You must believe me now, for here I stand.'
'His head it is supplies his lusty flesh
With all this lofty life and resurging.
Batter it then and see if *that* survives;
And pulp his secret on the cobblestones.'

Portrayed again and this time on a boat
Hands tied behind his back, glazed figurehead
Breasting the wave with white flesh, cherry lips
And freshly glossy dark black cherry ringlets.
Figurehead for heroic acts, bright log
That faltering worshippers tie their goodness to.
So let the ship depart on its endless voyage
Cracked and warped as it is with the summer pestilence
That swells tongues in the back streets of the town
That bloats the corpses in the sewers thrown,
Ricocheting disease, flesh stuck to flesh
Clinging to what it takes its fever from.

So out to its plate of water where no land
Can ever creep up round the horizon, where salt
Dries out the festers, shrinks flesh, where the thongs crack
And Sebastian's hands burst free. Above his head
They soar, and like a swallow flashing
His body shoots from the deck. In a perfect dive
His encrusted body of death he draws through the green
Green wave. The mighty ocean takes him.
At last upon his proper element
Embarked, immersed in waters, laved in love
He can make use of all adversity.
Buoyed up with salt and love, O he rides over
Six little waves to roll in each seventh seventh.

'O all you worshippers, locked far inland
O you may keep the images of my flesh
And let help who it may; the rigours of love
I have gone through have freed me to a life
To use my body as I know it best,
Not bodiless adoration, but embodied
In every turn and twist, the dolphin's lair,
Directed by the thinking heart, so now
I run with the tide, and this great tide runs high,
This is true worship, to breathe, to act, to be
Part of this running tide, in love set free.'

The much-garbed painted crowd cling to each other
Pointing and looking at the empty hill for their saint.
Far off between the hills at the end of the picture
The noonday sun sparkles on the little waves.

# ANNE STEVENSON

**Anne Stevenson** was born in England of American parents in 1933, but when she was six-months-old her parents returned with her to America. She grew up in New England and in Ann Arbor, Michigan, where she went to high school and university. After studying music and languages at Michigan, she returned to England where – with the exception of a period in the American south and visits to Massachusetts and Vermont – she has lived ever since. She now lives in Langley Park, Co. Durham.

Her six books of poems include four published by Oxford University Press: *Correspondences* (1974), *Travelling Behind Glass* (1974), *Enough of Green* (1977) and *Minute by Glass Minute* (1982). She has also published a study of the American poet Elizabeth Bishop. A new collection, *The Fiction Makers,* will appear from Oxford in 1985, and a *Selected Poems* in 1986.

I was born in England about the time Hitler came into power and Franklin Roosevelt was first elected president of the United States. My American parents, who had met in a Cincinnati high school, were then living in Cambridge while my father studied philosophy under I.A. Richards and Wittgenstein and my mother steeped herself in Bloomsbury and Gibbon. But my arrival (and Hitler's) brought their English honeymoon to an end. When I was six-months-old they took me back to Massachusetts; from there we moved to New Haven where my father taught philosophy and mathematics. During the war he wrote a book, *Ethics and Language*, which earned him sudden dismissal from Yale. We retreated to California for a summer, and then lived in Chicago before we settled in Ann Arbor, Michigan, where I went to high school and university.

My childhood was happy but bewildered. Philosophy of a some-what stern, analytical nature was my father's profession, but I remember him chiefly as a pianist (we always had two pianos and a number of cellos) and as a superb reader of poetry. My mother, a tender and intelligent woman, wrote fiction herself and spent hours reading aloud to us – R.L. Stevenson, Walter Scott, George MacDonald, Dickens, Mark Twain. During long summer vacations my sister Diana and I played *The Black Arrow, The Princess and the Goblin,* or *A Tale of Two Cities* on our front porch and up and down the pear tree in our back garden. What I chiefly remember from those days is wanting to live in a story. If only I could have been a boy! Then I could have run away to sea; or I could have been a Great Composer like Mozart the Wonder Child; or I could have been a troubadour.

In those early years in New Haven it never occurred to me that school could be anything but irrelevant, so I happily accepted the role of "dullest in the class" until, in the sixth grade, I had a teacher who made us learn poems by heart. To my amazement I found I could learn lines and recite them. Poetry was something I could *do*, like playing the piano and cello and making up "plays" for my friends. Until I was eighteen or nineteen I took it for granted that I would become a musician, but in high school I began to prefer acting, and at the University of Michigan I remember deciding coolly that writing was an art which endured, while acting and playing music were secondary and ephemeral; I would be a writer. I began to write my own variety of Elizabethan lyric – a masque for dancers called *The Silver Heron* and libretto for a one-act opera, *Adam and Eve and The Devil.* Both of these were performed at Michigan, but even then I knew that my artist/dancer/composer friends were curiously out of touch with "reality". We dreamed of pre-war Paris, of Bohemian garrets and the ghettos of Modernism.

When I left Michigan I was intoxicated with the idea of becoming an artist. At the same time I thirsted for "real life", and assumed that any story I lived could be incorporated into the fiction I intended to make of myself. I came to England to marry a childhood playmate who had been seconded to New Haven during the war. When we met as adults, he seemed glamorous, a conflation of Rupert Brooke and Robin Hood. Marriage, I thought, would be the culmination of my American success story. I was secretly relieved not to have to think of a career in writing or teaching.

But that marriage was not a success. We were both self-centred and ambitious; and society was shifting its shape all around us. As for England, I scarcely saw it for my idealised picture of it. When I began to write, I had no language to express what I did not know. Until I was divorced and returned with my daughter to take an M.A. at Michigan, I continually mistook the accoutrements of art for the truths of life. Even then I indulged in Romantic imaginings. It took me two unhappy marriages and three children to make me reconsider my assumptions.

I returned to an America stripped of safety, early in the 1960s. My mother was dying of cancer. My four-year-old daughter was a source of love and agony and guilt. I was full of self-doubt and bitterness. But, with encouragement from Donald Hall at Michigan, I began to write poems again – no longer Elizabethan lyrics, but sad, sometimes cynical poems in the shadow of Robert Frost, Richard Wilbur and, when I'd discovered her, Elizabeth Bishop. Hall got me a "commission" (without money) to write a study of Elizabeth Bishop for Twayne's United States Authors Series. About the same time I decided against working for a Ph.D., and moved to Cambridge, Massachusetts, to teach at the Cambridge School of Weston.

In Cambridge I married again and finished my book on Elizabeth Bishop, with help from letters she wrote me from Brazil. That was the period of the Bay of Pigs, the Kennedy assassinations, hippies, beautiful people, marijuana, suicide and confusion – the 1960s, when America lost confidence in her virtue (chiefly in Vietnam) and a whole generation lost confidence in the future. With my English husband I went back to Cambridge, England to try being a wife again. I found myself a mother with a daughter and, subsequently, two sons. Yet I was still lost, footless, countryless, unable to feel my way into or out of the academic society (Cambridge, Glasgow, Oxford) in which my husband clearly belonged. It was not until I lived in Scotland, first in Glasgow, and then on the Tay estuary, with a lively Highland girl who shared a cottage with me, that I began to see my way through irrational miseries I could neither explain nor confront.

While I lived in Glasgow I finished *Correspondences*, an epistolary poem about an American family, not unlike my own, but *not* my own. Without resorting to confessional poetry, I managed to exorcise some of the guilt I felt with regard to my mother, my children, the nineteenth-century puritanical morality in which I'd grown up – and indeed, with regard to my confused, poisoned feelings about America itself. *Correspondences* was published in 1974, when I was writer in residence at Dundee University, as was a Selected Poems, named after a long poem I'd written in Glasgow, *Travelling Behind Glass*.

In Dundee I made many friends. I liked and still like the Scots. Theirs is a poetry of steely, philosophical romanticism, a good antidote to the soft-centred confessional stuff I'd been drawn into in America. In Dundee we laughed and drank and behaved in a generally anarchic (Celtic) manner, but we never felt pity for ourselves. I wrote most of *Enough of Green* when I was living in Tayport, before I moved south to a fellowship at Lady Margaret Hall in Oxford.

I came to Oxford intending to take up my marriage from where we'd left it, uneasily, in Glasgow. I was now in a safe position, I thought, to write an authoritative academic book on American puritanism and be the faithful mother I thought I should be. As it turned out, I did neither of these things. The marriage seemed to belong to somebody else; and the academic book never materialised; I had written enough about puritans in *Correspondences*. In March 1979 my father died suddenly in Vermont. In October, Elizabeth Bishop died in New York. Between those two dates, I had moved away from Oxford and, with Michael Farley, started The Poetry Bookshop in Hay-on-Wye on the Hereford/Wales border. This precarious venture was too frailly financed to produce any profit (although it is doing well today under Alan Halsey) but it brought Michael and myself to Wales and forced me to re-evaluate, once again, all I believed to be the case – about art and life and my own irresolute, unpredictable way through the world. In Hay it became clear to me that the only literary tradition I could honestly attach myself to would be a religious tradition; and that tradition, in my time, seemed scarcely to exist. Yet everything else I had tried to do or be seemed false, wrong, blind, selfish, or impulsively giddy. The poems I wrote in Hay were a response to a certain kind of natural beauty, but they were also poems of dazed discovery and, of course, anxiety.

I suspect I share with many Welsh poets, as I do with some Scottish poets, a sense that poetry must in some way be a celebration, an act of praise, a gesture of reconciliation – what David Jones called a 'making'. That God makes and that man makes in the image of God (Jones's cardinal belief) is quite a different notion from that I gleaned from my American education, which put responsibility for self-making heavily in one's own hands. I was brought up in a tradition of self-improvement, self-pity and self-advertising. First in Scotland and later in Wales, it began to sink in on me that 'I' is not the best foundation upon which to build an art. Any art needs a tradition, a history, a mythology, a faith. The religious work-ethic in America (as in many places in Europe) has led to the rule of technocrats and capitalists, a process I tried to trace in *Correspondences* in which religious attitudes are corrupted by self-interest until they lead to personal and social breakdown. But there is another way of going about things, what one might call a "work-aesthetic" in which an artist commits himself (herself) to craft almost at the expense of self. Guided by Jones (I find his poetry less accessible than his creed, while I find Yeats's poetry an inspiration *despite* his creed) I have tried to use the strong visual experience recorded in poems like 'Buzzard and Alder' as a source of crafted poems – to lay, as it were, on the altar of making.

I am not, as David Jones was, much of a scholar; nor am I as single-minded as I think an artist should be. But I am, and always have been, a pilgrim. Much of what passes for poetry these days seems to me trivial, self-regarding games-playing; cleverness for cleverness's sake – or for the poet's sake. But I no longer want to play the literary game. I had enough of that in Oxford. I believe I wouldn't mind if I never published another poem, so long as I felt I could continue the pilgrimage in *some* art. Poetry has so far been the best way of 'making' I've found. But prose might do as well. Or prayer, which is most difficult of all.

In 1981/82 I was appointed Northern Arts Literary Fellow and moved to Sunderland where Michael Farley had been asked to edit books for Ceolfrith Press. Circumstances forced us to sell our large Sunderland house and move to an ex-colliery village near Durham. Here Michael has established Taxvs Press in the David Jones tradition (man-the-artist/man-the-priest). But it is important to understand that there is nothing pietistic about an attitude which regards the making of signs or sacraments central to a poetic tradition. We live in barbarian times. Technocracy surrounds us, infiltrating our most meagre assumptions, corrupting the five-year-old child as it does the most remote hill farmer and the most conspicuous politician.

No artist can be optimistic in days of spiritual decay, but it is possible to be honest. And joyful. In these days of superfluous affluence, rewarded wickedness and sophisticated violence, my answer is to live simply, reducing my needs to the level of the beautiful and the necessary. From a position of having much and little, it is possible to live more richly than I ever imagined.

ANNE STEVENSON

## Transparencies
*A Letter to My Sons*


Your time with me ends with August, and now
August is over. Between Oxford and Cambridge –
that English triangle they make with London –
fields must be yellow harvested, as here in Wales.
Little straw-built cities, movable dolmens.
They look solid enough to believe in, stacked in bales.
    I carry my wound back upright in the car
    as if its grief could spill.

But it's a gift, too, this grief-grail, freedom to
love you without you. 'My sons' creates you abstract as
gold fields the windows slide behind your faces,
crossing by bus to grandparents whose good sense
still can't splinter to forgiveness, who'll find you,
like your music, alien as energy. And all they have.
    Later you'll look past me and your cleft childhood
    to their calm, whole house

where habit and reason – harvest of half a century's
lesson in upheaval – look solid enough to believe in,
if, by then, abstractions like 'the past' and 'mother'
make you cry – and like to cry. The act of memory's
a film we learn to make and watch so lives
can be performances. Worse than TV –
    to leave your tea mugs and *The Moon of Gomrath*
    plangent on a table

and, as if you were here, set off with the dog
to the riverpath, where yesterday the sun
struck slantwise, shafted, just as now. I see how
last year's leaves are almost this year's dust.
Papery thorn shapes . . . maple . . . alder . . . stir
in a gust of passing. Molecular squall of gnats
    where the path's still hot. Leaves like syllables
    of light in a text of shadows.

This is a letter I'd never write if I could
send you counsel. Cicero, Polonius – thistles
preaching their beards to their blown seed. Oh,

it's your particular selves I need to hold
to the light as you cross the impossible lens of now
and now. Solid enough to believe . . . until
    the river ripples under your melting faces
    mouthing at me from its thin windows.


## The Victory

I thought you were my victory
though you cut me like a knife
when I brought you out of my body
into your life.

Tiny antagonist, gory,
blue as a bruise. The stains
of your cloud of glory
bled from my veins.

How can you dare, blind thing,
blank insect eyes?
You barb the air. You sting
with bladed cries.

Snail! Scary knot of desires!
Hungry snarl! Small son.
Why do I have to love you?
How have you won?


## Generations

Know this mother by her three smiles.
One grey one drawn over her mouth by frail hooks.
One hurt smile under each eye.

Know this mother by the frames she makes.
By the silence in which she suffers each child
to scratch out the aquatints in her mind.

Know this mother by the way she says
"darling" with her teeth clenched.
By the fabulous lies she cooks.


## The Mother

Of course I love them, they are my children.
That is my daughter and this my son.
And this is my life I give them to please them.
It has never been used. Keep it safe. Pass it on.


## After the End of It

You gave and gave,
and now you say you're poor.
I'm in your debt, you say,
and there's no way to repay you
but by my giving more.

Your pound of flesh is what you must have?
Here's what I've saved.

This sip of wine is yours,
this sieve of laughter. Yours,
too, these broken haloes
from my cigarette, these coals
that flicker when the salt wind howls
and the letter box blinks like a loud
eyelid over the empty floor.

I'll send this, too, this gale between rains,
this wild day. Its cold is so cold
I want to break it into panes
like new ice on a pond; then pay it
pain by pain to your account.
Let it freeze us both into some numb country!
Giving and taking might be the same there.
A future of measurement and blame
gone in a few bitter minutes.

## The Garden

She feels it like a shoulder of hair,
the garden, shrugging off the steamed, squeezed
eye of her kitchen window. Self-engendered chaos,
milky convolvulus, huge comet daisies. Tear
open the stocking of the leek pod and it frees
mathematically its globe, its light radiants.

But still she feels it hateful, August in its sweat,
the children filthy and barefoot . . . angry woman
in a stained striped apron, sipping juice off a knife,
thick syrups of pounded rose hip and pulped fruit.
In bright air, between briar roses and a viney drain.
*Arenea diadema* sips the silk-spindled fly.

Her pet cat's a killer, a fur muff
curled fatly now in a catnest of hot
grass and goutweed. Of this morning's robin
too much was left – feathers, fluff
feet, beak, the gorgeous throat caught
in the gored, delicate, perfectly balanced skeleton.


## Sonnets for Five Seasons

### This House

which represents you, as my bones do, waits
all pores open, for the stun of snow. Which will come
as it always does, between breaths, between nights
of no wind and days of the nulled sun.
And has to be welcome. All instinct wants to anticipate
faceless fields, a white road drawn
through dependent firs, the soldered glare of lakes.

Is it wanting you here to want the winter in?
I breathe you back into your square house and begin
to live here roundly. This year will be between,
not in, four seasons. Do you hear already the wet
rumble of thaw? Stones. Sky. Streams.
Sun. Those might be swallows at the edge of sight
returning to last year's nest in the crook of the porchlight.

## Complaint

'Dear God', they write, 'that was a selfish winter
to lean so long, unfairly, on the spring.
And now – this too much greed of seedy summer.
Mouths of the flowers unstick themselves and sting
the bees with irresistible dust. Iris
allow undignified inspection. Plain waste
weeds dress up in Queen Anne's lace; our mist
blue sky clouds heavily with clematis –

'Too much' they cry, 'too much. Begin again.'
The Lord, himself a casualty of weather,
falls to earth in large hot drops of rain.
The dry loam rouses in his scent, and under
him – moist, sweet, discriminate – the spring.
Thunder. Lightning. He can do anything.

## Between

The wet and weight of this half-born English winter
is not the weather of those fragmentary half-true willows
that break in the glass of the canal behind our rudder
as water arrives in our wake – a travelling arrow
of now, of now, of now. Leaves of the water
furl back from our prow, and as the pinnate narrow
seam of where we are drives through the mirror
of where we have to be, alder and willow
double crookedly, reverse, assume a power
to bud out tentatively in gold and yellow, so
it looks as if what should be end of summer –
seeds, dead nettles, berries, naked boughs –
is really the anxious clouding of first spring.
. . . 'Real' is what water is imagining.

## Stasis

Before the leaves change, light transforms these lucid
speaking trees. The heavy drench of August
alters, thins; its rich and sappy blood
relaxes where a thirst ago, no rest
released the roots' wet greed or stemmed their mad
need to be more. September is the wisest

time – neither the unbearable burning word
nor the form of it, cooped in its cold ghost.

How are they sombre – that unpicked apple, red,
undisturbed by its fall; calm of those wasp-bored amethyst
plums on the polished table? Body and head
easy in amity, a beam between that must,
unbalanced, quicken or kill, make new or dead
whatever these voices are that hate the dust.


*The Circle*

It is imagination's white face remembers
snow, its shape, a fluted shell on shoot
or flower, its weight, the permanence of winter
pitched against the sun's absolute root.

All March is shambles, shards. Yet no amber
chestnut, Indian, burnished by its tent
cuts to a cleaner centre or keeps a summer
safer in its sleep. Ghost, be content.

You died in March when white air hurt the maples.
Birches knelt under ice. Roads forgot
their way in aisles of frost. There were no petals.

Face, white face, you are snow in the green hills.
High stones complete your circle where trees start.
Granite and ice are colours of the heart.


*From* **Green Mountain, Black Mountain**

After April snow,
such a green thaw.
A chiff-chaff chips a warmer home
in that cloud-cliff.
The river bulges,
flexing brown Japanese muscles,
moving its smooth planes in multitudes.
Threads of white melt stitch
the slashed flanks of the hill fields.

Soon the animal will be well again,
hunting and breeding
in grass-covered bones.
It peers from these clinical windows
apprehensive but healing.
To be whole would be enough.
To be whole and well and warm,
content with a kill.


## Swifts

Spring comes little, a little. All April it rains.
The new leaves stick in their fists. New ferns, still fiddleheads.
But one day the swifts are back. Face to the sun like a child
You shout, 'The swifts are back!'

Sure enough, bolt nocks bow to carry one sky-scyther
Two hundred miles an hour across fullblown windfields.
*Swreeeee. Swreeee.* Another. And another.
It's the cut air falling in shrieks on our chimneys and roofs.

The next day, a fleet of high crosses cruises in ether.
These are the air pilgrims, pilots of air rivers . . .
But a shift of wing and they're earth-skimmers, daggers,
Skilful in guiding the throw of themselves away from themselves.

Quick flutter, a scimitar upsweep, out of danger of touch, for
Earth is forbidden to them, water's forbidden to them.
All air and fire, little owlish ascetics, they outfly storms.
They rush to the pillars of altitude, the thermal fountains.

Here is a legend of swifts, a parable –
When the great Raven bent over earth to create the birds
The swifts were ungrateful. They were small muddy things
Like shoes, with long legs and short wings, so

They took themselves off to the mountains to sulk.
And they stayed there. 'Well,' said the Raven, after years of this,
'I will give you the sky, you can have the whole sky
On condition that you give up rest.'

'Yes, yes,' screamed the swifts. 'We abhor rest.
We detest the filth of growth, the sweat of sleep,
Soft nests in the wet fields, slimehold of worms.
Let us be free, be air!'

So the Raven took their legs and bound them into their bodies.
He bent their wings like boomerangs, honed them like knives.
He streamlined their feathers and stripped them of velvet.
Then he released them, *Never to Return*

Inscribed on their feet and wings. And so
We have swifts, though in reality not parables but
Bolts in the world's need, swift
Swifts, not in punishment, not in ecstasy, simply

Sleepers over oceans in the mill of the world's breathing.
The grace to say they live in another firmament.
A way to say the miracle will not occur,
And watch the miracle.


## Buzzard and Alder

Buzzard that folds itself into and becomes nude
alder; alder that insensibly becomes bird –
one life inside the dazzling tree. Together
they do change everything, and forever.

You think, because no news is said here,
not. But rain's rained weather to a rare
blue, so you can see the thinness of it,
I mean the layer they live in, flying in it,

breaking through it minute by glass minute.
Buzzard, hunched in disuse before it
shatters winter, wheeling after food.
Alder, silently glazing us, the dead.

## Small Philosophical Poem

Dr Animus, whose philosophy is a table,
sits down contentedly to a square meal.
The plates lie there, and there,
just where they should lie.
His feet stay just where they should stay,
between legs and the floor.
His eyes believe the clean waxed surfaces
are what they are.

But while he's eating his un-
exceptional propositions, his wise
wife Anima, sweeping a haze-gold decanter
from a metaphysical salver,
pours him a small glass of doubt.
Just what he needs.
He smacks his lips and cracks his knuckles.
The world is the pleasure of thought.

He'd like to stay awake all night
(elbows on the table)
talking of how the table might not be there.
But Anima, whose philosophy is hunger,
perceives the plates are void in empty air.
The floor is void beneath his trusting feet.
Peeling her glass from its slender cone of fire
she fills the room with love. And fear. And fear.

# FLEUR ADCOCK

**Fleur Adcock** was born in 1934 in Papakura, New Zealand. She grew up in New Zealand and in England (where she went to several schools during the war). After reading Classics at Victoria University, Wellington, she emigrated to Britain in 1963, and worked as a librarian until 1979. She is now a freelance writer, and lives in London.

Fleur Adcock's *Selected Poems* (Oxford University Press, 1983) includes work from six previous collections, four published by Oxford: *Tigers* (1967), *High Tide in the Garden* (1971), *The Scenic Route* (1974) and *The Inner Harbour* (1979). It also includes the Lake District poems of *Below Loughrigg* (Bloodaxe, 1979).

*The Virgin & the Nightingale*, Fleur Adcock's verse translations of medieval Latin poets, appeared from Bloodaxe in 1983. She also contributed translations to *The Greek Anthology* (Penguin Classics). Her *Oxford Book of Contemporary New Zealand Poetry* was published in 1982.

It never occurred to me when I was a child that writing poetry was not something women did – after all, Enid Blyton wrote poetry, didn't she? Or at least the *Sunny Stories* magazines our mother let us buy rather than comics contained little verses about fairies and flowers. These were the topics I myself wrote about at seven and eight, before I moved on to explorers, adventures and love.

I grew older, and my models improved. Much of my childhood was spent in England, where there really were woods with wild flowers in them, and the events of *A Midsummer Night's Dream* could still be convincingly imagined; but by my teens I had returned to New Zealand, another landscape altogether. My school was Wellington Girls' College; it had been Katherine Mansfield's school too, and Robin Hyde's – both tough, imaginative women, and neither deterred by her sex from writing. But now the poets I read were male: Blake, Milton, Eliot, Rilke. If I thought about this at all I regarded it as a mere historical accident: poets had happened for some centuries to be men; well, so had scientists and doctors and professors, until recently. It wasn't going to stop *me*. And after all, novelists were often women. Poetry or prose, I didn't mind which I wrote: both, ideally.

One of the characteristics of the young is their conviction of their own uniqueness: it was impossible to see myself as the product of my time and circumstances; I was *me*, there would never be another exactly the same, I was going to *show* them. My poems of that time are full not only of adolescent despair and introspection but of seething ambition: just you wait, they say. Later, with more experience, came more humility, but the determination persisted.

Perhaps there was something to be said, after all, for beginning one's poetic career in New Zealand: New Zealand poetry had scarcely moved out of its imitative, colonial, pseudo-English phase until the 1930s; most of the New Zealand poets there had ever been were still alive and writing during the time I was learning to write myself, at school and at university and for a few years afterwards. I was only twenty or thirty years behind the pioneers. I knew some of them – I even married a poet; to compete seemed a not impossible ambition.

Motherhood is often said (by men) to serve as a substitute for creativity. Possibly it explains why I wrote so few poems during my marriage; or perhaps I was inhibited by being married to a "real" poet; or perhaps I was simply too busy, first as a married student and then as a student and a mother. Alistair helped a lot with the first baby, but by the time the second one arrived we were drifting apart. At twenty-four I was in Dunedin, divorced and at last independent. I made friends of my own – many of them writers – and with long solitary evenings to myself I got on with learning the craft. Those four years created in me an addiction to solitude which I have never shaken off: I was still a mother, but I was no longer part of an accepted social unit; I had become, in a way unlike anything my adolescent self had envisaged, me. Even now, in spite of the evidence I see, I find it hard to imagine how anyone, but particularly a woman, can be both a domestic partner and a writer – how would she find time to *think*?

Eventually, like Katherine Mansfield and Robin Hyde, I found New Zealand stifling; in 1963 I escaped to London, with my younger son. I had never intended to be a New Zealander, and it was not until I was back in England that I found I had become one. I experienced culture shock for the second time in my life, but now it was accompanied by excitement and a sense of the world opening out instead of closing in. Gradually and inevitably I adapted, until I reached a state in which New Zealanders of the new nationalistic breed now scorn me as a Pom. Fair enough: the country of my birth feels deeply foreign to me after more than twenty years away from it.

The question of my nationality has always seemed at least as significant as the question of my gender. I write a good deal about places; I have passionate relationships with them. Wherever I happen to live I have always some residual feeling of being an outsider: a fruitful position for a writer, perhaps, if it means one takes nothing for granted. But now I wonder: has being a woman contributed to this? Are women natural outsiders? Perhaps my early competitiveness had something to do with being female, as well as being young.

For much of my working life, both as a librarian in the Civil Service and as a poet, I was surrounded by men; it took me rather a long time to discover the rewards and pleasures of female company. In my early poems there were few women apart from fabulised or fictionalised versions of myself; the men and the children were real, because I knew about men and children, but I had to play most of the female roles myself. My more recent poems are full of women and girls, real or imaginary, seen from inside or outside, all of them at some time sufficiently interesting to me for the poems to have got written. I do have the impression that women in general have become more interesting; and certainly more of them are writing poetry. But if society has changed, so have I. I used to enjoy being the token woman at poetry readings; now I enjoy finding that there are so many of us. The once tediously frequent question of whether women can "really" be poets already sounds old-fashioned.

FLEUR ADCOCK

## Stewart Island

'But look at all this beauty'
said the hotel manager's wife
when asked how she could bear to
live there. True: there was a fine bay,
all hills and atmosphere; white
sand, and bush down to the sea's edge;
oyster-boats, too, and Maori
fishermen with Scottish names (she
ran off with one that autumn).
As for me, I walked on the beach;
it was too cold to swim. My
seven-year-old collected shells
and was bitten by sandflies;
my four-year-old paddled, until
a mad seagull jetted down
to jab its claws and beak into
his head. I had already
decided to leave the country.

## Kilpeck

We are dried and brittle this morning,
fragile with continence, quiet.
You have brought me to see a church.
I stare at a Norman arch in red sandstone
carved like a Mayan temple-gate;
at serpents writhing up the doorposts
and squat saints with South-American features
who stare back over our heads
from a panel of beasts and fishes.
The gargoyles jutting from under the eaves
are the colour of newborn children.

Last night you asked me
if poetry was the most important thing.

We walk on around the building
craning our heads back to look up

at lions, griffins, fat-faced bears.
The Victorians broke some of these figures
as being too obscene for a church;
but they missed the Whore of Kilpeck.
She leans out under the roof
holding her pink stony cleft agape
with her ancient little hands.
There was always witchcraft here, you say.

The sheep-track up to the fragments
of castle-wall is fringed with bright bushes.
We clamber awkwardly, separate.
Hawthorn and dogrose offer hips and haws,
orange and crimson capsules, pretending
harvest. I taste a blackberry.
The soil here is coloured like brick-dust,
like the warm sandstone. A fruitful county.
We regard it uneasily.

There is little left to say
after all the talk we had last night
instead of going to bed—
fearful for our originality,
avoiding the sweet obvious act
as if it were the only kind of indulgence.
Silly, perhaps.
                                We have our reward.
We are languorous now, heavy
with whatever we were conserving,
carrying each a delicate burden
of choices made or about to be made.
Words whisper hopefully in our heads.

Slithering down the track we hold hands
to keep a necessary balance.
The gargoyles extend their feral faces,
rosy, less lined than ours.
We are wearing out our identities.

# Things

There are worse things than having behaved foolishly in public.
There are worse things than these miniature betrayals,
committed or endured or suspected; there are worse things
than not being able to sleep for thinking about them.
It is 5 a.m. All the worse things come stalking in
and stand icily about the bed looking worse and worse and worse.

## Below Loughrigg

The power speaks only out of sleep and blackness
no use looking for the sun
what is not present cannot be illumined

Katherine's lungs, remember, eaten by disease
but Mary's fingers too
devoured and she goes on writing

The water speaks from the rocks, the cavern speaks,
where water halloos through it
this happens also in darkness

A steep bit here, up from the valley
to the terraces, the path eroded by water
Now listen for the voice

These things wane with the vital forces
he said, little having waned in him
except faith, and anger had replaced it

One force can be as good as another
we may not think so; but channelled
in ways it has eaten out; issuing

into neither a pool nor the sea
but a shapely lake afloat with wooded islands
a real water and multiplied on maps

which can be read in the sunlight; for the sun
will not be stopped from visiting
and the lake exists and the wind sings over it.

## Madmen

Odd how the seemingly maddest of men –
sheer loonies, the classically paranoid,
violently possessive about their secrets,
whispered after from corners, terrified
of poison in their coffee, driven frantic
(whether for or against him) by discussion of God,
peculiar, to say the least, about their mothers –
return to their gentle senses in bed.

Suddenly straightforward, they perform
with routine confidence, neither afraid
that their partner will turn and bite their balls off
nor groping under the pillow for a razor-blade;
eccentric only in their conversation,
which rambles on about the meaning of a word
they used in an argument in 1969,
they leave their women grateful, relieved, and bored.

## Blue Glass

*analagous with melanies experience*

The underworld of children becomes the overworld
when Janey or Sharon shuts the attic door
on a sunny afternoon and tiptoes in sandals
that softly waffle-print the dusty floor

to the cluttered bed below the skylight,
managing not to sneeze as she lifts
newspapers, boxes, gap-stringed tennis-racquets
and a hamster's cage to the floor, and shifts

the tasselled cover to make a clean surface
and a pillow to be tidy under her head
before she straightens, mouths the dark sentence,
and lays herself out like a mummy on the bed.

Her wrists are crossed. The pads of her fingertips
trace the cold glass emblem where it lies
like a chain of hailstones melting in the dips
above her collarbones. She needs no eyes

to see it: the blue bead necklace, of sapphire
or lapis, or of other words she knows
which might mean blueness: amethyst, azure,
chalcedony can hardly say how it glows.

She stole it. She tells herself that she found it.
It's hers now. It owns her. She slithers among
its globular teeth, skidding on blue pellets.
Ice-beads flare and blossom on her tongue,

turn into flowers, populate the spaces
around and below her. The attic has become
her bluebell wood. Among their sappy grasses
the light-fringed gas-flames of bluebells hum.

They lift her body like a cloud of petals.
High now, floating, this is what she sees:
granular bark six inches from her eyeballs;
the wood of rafters is the wood of trees.

Her breathing moistens the branches' undersides;
the sunlight in an interrupted shaft
warms her legs and lulls her as she rides
on air, a slender and impossible raft

of bones and flesh; and whether it is knowledge
or a limpid innocence on which she feeds
for power hasn't mattered. She turns the necklace
kindly in her fingers, and soothes the beads.


## Instructions to Vampires

I would not have you drain
With your sodden lips the flesh that has fed mine,
And leech his bubbling blood to a decline:
Not that pain;

Nor visit on his mind
That other desiccation, where the wit
Shrivels: so to be humbled is not fit
For his kind.

But use acid or flame,
Secretly, to brand or cauterize;
And on the soft globes of his mortal eyes
Etch my name.


## A Way Out

The other option's to become a bird.
That's kindly done, to guess from how they sing,
decently independent of the word
as we are not; and how they use the air
to sail as we might soaring on a swing
higher and higher; but the rope's not there,

it's free fall upward, out into the sky;
or if the arc veer downward, then it's planned:
a bird can loiter, skimming just as high
as lets him supervise the hazel copse,
the turnip field, the orchard, and then land
on just the twig he's chosen. Down he drops

to feed, if so it be: a pretty killer,
a keen-eyed stomach weighted like a dart.
He feels no pity for the caterpillar,
that moistly munching hoop of innocent green.
It is such tender lapses twist the heart.
A bird's heart is a tight little red bean,

untwistable. His beak is made of bone,
his feet apparently of stainless wire;
his coat's impermeable; his nest's his own.
The clogging multiplicity of things
amongst which other creatures, battling, tire
can be evaded by a pair of wings.

The point is, most of it occurs below,
earthed at the levels of the grovelling wood
and gritty buildings. Up's the way to go.
If it's escapist, if it's like a dream
the dream's prolonged until it ends for good.
I see no disadvantage in the scheme.

## Bogyman

Stepping down from the blackberry bushes
he stands in my path: Bogyman.
He is not as I had remembered him,
though he still wears the broad-brimmed hat,
the rubber-soled shoes and the woollen gloves.
No face; and that soft mooning voice
still spinning its endless distracting yarn.

But this is daylight, a misty autumn
Sunday, not unpopulated
by birds. I can see him in such colours
as he wears – fawn, grey, murky blue –
not all shadow-clothed, as he was that night
when I was ten; he seems less tall
(I have grown) and less muffled in silence.

I have no doubt at all, though, that he is
Bogyman. He is why children
do not sleep all night in their tree-houses.
He is why, when I had pleaded
to spend a night on the common, under
a cosy bush, and my mother
surprisingly said yes, she took no risk.

He was the risk I would not take: better
to make excuses, to lose face,
than to meet the really faceless, the one
whose name was too childish for us
to utter – 'murderers' we talked of, and
'lunatics escaped from Earlswood'.
But I met him, of course, as we all do.

Well, that was then; I survived; and later
survived meetings with his other
forms, bold or pathetic or disguised – the
slummocking figure in a dark
alley, or the lover turned suddenly
icy-faced; fingers at my throat
and ludicrous violence in kitchens.

H

I am older now, and (I tell myself,
circling carefully around him
at the far edge of the path, pretending
I am not in fact confronted)
can deal with such things. But what, Bogyman,
shall I be at twice my age? (At
your age?) Shall I be grandmotherly, fond

suddenly of gardening, chatty with
neighbours? Or strained, not giving in,
writing for *Ambit* and hitch-hiking to
Turkey? Or sipping Guinness in
the Bald-Faced Stag, in wrinkled stockings? Or
(and now I look for the first time
straight at you) something like you, Bogyman?


## Crab


Late at night we wrench open a crab;
flesh bursts out of its cup

in pastel colours. The dark fronds attract me:
Poison, you say, Dead Men's Fingers –

don't put them in your mouth, stop!
They brush over my tongue, limp and mossy,

until you snatch them from me, as you snatch
yourself, gently, if I come too close.

Here are the permitted parts of the crab,
wholesome on their nests of lettuce

and we are safe again in words.
All day the kitchen will smell of sea.

## Three Rainbows in One Morning

It is not only the eye that is astonished.

Predictable enough in rainbow weather,
the drenched air saturated with colours,
that over each valley should hang an arc
and over this long lake the longest.

Knowing how it happens is no defence.
They stop the car and are delighted.

But some centre of gravity is upset,
some internal gauge or indicator
fed once again with the routine question
'This place, now: would it be possible
to live here?' buzzes, rolls
and registers 'Yes. Yes; perhaps.'


## Mary Magdalene and the Birds

1

Tricks and tumbles are my trade; I'm
all birds to all men.
I switch voices, adapt my features,
do whatever turn you fancy.
All that is constant is my hair:

plumage, darlings, beware of it.

2

Blackbird: that's the one to watch —
or he is, with his gloss and weapon.
Not a profession for a female,
his brown shadow. Thrush is better,
cunning rehearser among the leaves,
and speckle-breasted, maculate.

3

A wound of some kind. All that talk
of the pelican, self-wounding,
feeding his brood from an ever-bleeding
bosom turns me slightly sick.

But seriousness can light upon
the flightiest. This tingling ache,
nicer than pain, is a blade-stroke:
not my own, but I let it happen.

4

What is balsam? What is nard?
Sweetnesses from the sweet life,
obsolete, fit only for wasting.

I groom you with this essence. Wash it
down the drain with tears and water.
We are too human. Let it pass.

5

*With my body I thee worship:*
breast on stone lies the rockdove
cold on that bare nest, cooing
its low call, unlulled,
restless for the calling to cease.

6

Mary Magdalene sang in the garden.
It was a swansong, said the women,
for his downdrift on the river.

It sounded more of the spring curlew
or a dawn sky full of larks,
watery trillings you could drown in.

# JENI COUZYN

**Jeni Couzyn** was born in South Africa in 1942. She grew up in Johannesburg, and read English and Drama at the University of Natal. In 1965 she emigrated to Britain. From 1975 to 1978 she lived in Canada, where she published three books and became a Canadian citizen. She now lives in London.

Her first book of poems, *Flying*, appeared from Workshop Press in 1970, and she has since published six other books, including *Monkeys' Wedding* (Cape, 1972; Heinemann, 1978), *Christmas in Africa* (Heinemann, 1975), and *House of Changes* (Heinemann, 1978). In 1983 *Life by Drowning: Selected Poems* appeared from Anansi in Canada and David Philip in South Africa. An updated *Life by Drowning* is published by Bloodaxe at the same time as this anthology.

ABOVE: *Jeni Couzyn with Anne Stevenson, Ruth Fainlight and Jenny Joseph at the National Poetry Centre in London, November 1984.*

I love poetry because of the precision of "opaque" language, where the word has its own substance, and one can hold it, turn it over, feel its weight. I love the music of words ringing together, and most of all the beautiful unfolding of meaning in symbol and image. Poetry is the oldest doorway in my life to understanding – within the configuration of words a still place where I can feel the pulse of truth at any one moment (for truth can only be of the moment, and yesterday's poem never fulfills me today).

I feel, with Walt Whitman in his poem 'As I Ebb'd with the Ocean of Life':

> Oppress'd with myself that I have dared to open my mouth,
> Aware now that amid all that blab whose echoes recoil upon me I have
>     not once had the least idea who or what I am,
> But that before all my arrogant poems the real Me stands yet untouch'd,
>     untold, altogether unreach'd

At this moment as I write, I hear the birds through the open window, and I hear their song *in* my body, my cells opening to make space for earth-life within the boundaries of my sensation. The experience is one of joy, yet because the task is to live within the *world*, I look for words and images to express the feeling:

> there is nothing in me but birdsong
> liquid and cool through my being –
> earth's sweet capillaries . . .

The words, the music, the images of the poem are only valuable as stepping stones into the experience where there is no form, no division. The words are like the colour and form of the flower – but the experience is its perfume. Asked by a journalist whom I write *for*, I found myself answering, 'I write for God' – meaning I write for the deepest eye and ear within myself that I am able to reach.

When I was younger, I confused my love for the experience of recognition *within* a poem with the poem itself. Because of this I muddled poetry with identity, and caused myself pain. When my daughter was born I was forced to die to the idea of myself as poet. My need to write, and the impossibility of writing with a young child, caused me great anguish, as it has so many women before me. Yet my frustration never dulled the wonder I felt as I sat still for two years, gazing at the beauty of spirit within flesh, which was my daughter. As I watched the miraculous process unfolding, I knew that I was seeing the direct embodiment of what I'd been seeking all my life.

By the time she was old enough for me to resume work, all

ambition had been burned out of me. 'I am a poet' now belongs with all the other false statements I could make about myself: 'I am a woman of forty-two, I am this sort of person or that.' As I get older, I become emptier and emptier. I write poems when I write them, but I don't hold on to them. I am free of poetry.

Last Christmas I experienced the death of a close friend. During the weeks and months of her death, I saw the departure from her body of life, as I had seen its entry with my daughter's birth. I saw her, or rather, *experienced* her withdrawing into that place we call within, knowing it is not a place, but a state of being. On the morning of her death, I sat with her body for some hours, before the undertaker came. I felt no sadness. She was very much alive. If you ask *where* she was, I would have to say within me – because that is where I experienced her presence. Her children and close friends were crying in each other's arms. As I held the bodies I saw clearly that the "living" are animated corpses, little mechanical puppets for whom we, as being, are responsible. Some months later, during a high fever, I experienced a great cracking asunder, like a landmass breaking away from a continent. I can no longer confuse what I am with the doings of the puppet Jeni.

But the way I endeavour to live, and the poems I write, are a way *I as life* come through the Jeni into existence. There are times when my actions and thoughts are mechanical – the automatic action/ reaction of the robot brain. But when I am still and centred (as one must be when writing a poem), my deepest being which is my true self rises through the little self into existence. As the poems begin to harden into past, into substance, they slide off me, leaving me light and unencumbered with the identity of "poet".

Yet for me, poets do have a purpose. At best they are among the singers who come trooping into existence, bringing news of immortality into the projected substance of the world. Often they confuse themselves by serving little-self constructs, but beyond this personal service is the service to that energy which we call the "Muse" or the "Daemon" which represents, in my vocabulary, Angel, the One Woman, the One Man.

'Tell all the truth, but tell it slant' cautions Emily Dickinson, and Kathleen Raine writes to me along the same lines: 'Things about God need to be approached quietly.' Perhaps poems, because they enter the mind 'slant' are sometimes able to slip through the jabber of thought (not to be confused with *ideas* which, like poems, come out of stillness) directly into consciousness.

As a child, I read very little, though I wrote constantly from about the age of ten – poems that I kept in secret notebooks with cloth covers.

I was a solitary child, rebellious and defiant, challenging everything and everyone, yet always as I remember, afraid. Afraid of my parents, afraid of the dark, of malevolent spirits, of black burglars in the shadows and, later, of white policemen on the doorstep at dawn. I was born and brought up in South Africa, and it wasn't until I had found a space for myself as a young adult in England that the rich song of my South African childhood floated up into my consciousness, and expressed itself in images in my poems. The sound of crickets at evening, the hot sweet rustle of the veld, above all the hush and roar of the sea all entered my work.

Although as a schoolgirl I fell in love with teachers from time to time, there was never a teacher I could talk to about writing, and I didn't make a firm connection between literature and poems one wrote oneself, which were private and sacred. One experience stands out vividly from my high school years. I was just twelve, and rushed to school very excited one morning, to join my friends who were playing rounders on the playing field below the school. 'Quick,' I shouted, 'come and look at this!' With a stick I poked a dot on the dusty pink earth. 'That's the world,' I announced. Then I jabbed dots for several feet around it. 'That's the stars – all the stars we can see.' Then I pointed to the rest of the field, vast, stretching out to the fence, and the street beyond. 'Look! Look!' I shouted. They stared at me, glanced at each other shrugging and returned to their game.

When I was fifteen one of my sisters gave me two long-playing records of Dylan Thomas reading his own poems. I listened to them endlessly, absorbing his music. My other sister, who had just started university, pushed some lines of Edith Sitwell indignantly in front of me: 'You understand poetry. So tell me what this is supposed to mean?' *Lips like jangling pink rain. Lips like jangling pink rain.* And truly, in my ignorance, I tried to make sense of them, feeling a loyalty to poetry I couldn't have explained.

Africa for me was full of music. I remember sitting in my mother's kitchen peeling wild mushrooms, or shelling great mounds of green peas, with my mother and our servants and my sisters, singing songs in four harmonies, and feeling joy that was full of yearning.

After reading English at university, I met Lionel Abrahams and began to share my work for the first time. He published my poems in his magazine, and began to teach me about writing. I spent a few years producing plays with African children, writing poems and drinking cheap wine, talking late into the night with friends who were a motley bunch of artists, inhabitants of mental hospitals, political dissenters and alcoholics. Then I left for England.

My first poetry reading was at the Dublin Arts Club, chaired by that dear Irishman Padraic Colum, who wrote to me afterwards that I had 'a real lyrical talent'. It was only then that I began to think of poetry as a profession.

I began a precarious life in London as a "professional poet" that lasted ten years. Proud of the fact that I had "poet" stamped on my work permit, I lurched between triumph and despair, pain and joy, hate and love, walking always with death close beside me, yet holding to poetry as the central purpose of my life.

In 1975 I went to Canada on a reading tour, tried marriage (briefly) and became a Canadian citizen. Canada entered my wardrobe of identities – if I am South African then I am British and Canadian as well – if I am a poet, then I am a feminist, a therapist, and a mother. But I am none of these things. They are clothes the Jeni puts on, as I put on the Jeni.

JENI COUZYN

*From* **Christmas in Africa**
In the House of the Father


Christmas, the turning time, the final reckoning and the
forgiveness, we rode towards each year, over humps of
bitterness, towards the father

omnipotent and bountiful night rider with his magical
reindeer and sack full of gifts –
you could rely on him always to be there when you got there

accept the culmination of your year in his lap
hear all, forgive with a wish, and let you
begin all over;

a time of reprieve and new resolutions, time when you could
believe in new beginnings, a time of peace and long
playtime. With a hand in the dark

it began before dawn. The sun would rise over the city
as we passed the last gold hills of the mine dumps. Always
I saw children leaping up them, and in my head, in golden depths

a heap of little skeletons. Then the long hot hours dreaming
through the dorps each its single tree and tin roofs blazing
each its lone dog barking and black silent men

propped on the verandah of the general store, drinking
lemonade. Endless car games, the singing game chanting every
                    rhyme we knew
from ten green bottles to jesus loves me over the veld

to pass the time. At last, crossing, purple and lonely
the valley of a thousand hills, the tropical
deep smell of heavy flowers would glut the evening

and my father offered sixpence for the first to see the sea.
And there it was after a sudden unbending – that immense blue
                    promise.
Then inland into the sugar cane in the deep of night

the rustle of dunes and the sugar cane fields
the farmers who kept pythons fifty feet long to keep the rats down
and at midnight

the cottage. O the damp smell of foliage, smell of salt
and the sea's heavy breathing in the night, stray cries
of live things, batswing, shadows, sleep, and a ring of mornings.

The snakes were the price. In their hundreds they inhabited
our world at christmas. They were the hazard
in the garden. And they were everywhere

tangled in undergrowth, slithering over your feet in the pathway
stretched across doorways in the sun
lurking under the banana plant and nesting in the luckybean tree

they were everywhere, everywhere. And happiness was everywhere
in the father's time, who came down from heaven
in his red dressing gown and my father's shoes at the appointed time

cottonwool beard lopsided across his grin
his arms full of parcels.
His was the future that always came, keeping its promise.

In the house of the father the year would turn
a flower full blown, shedding its petals.
Glistened in your hand a free gift, a clean seed.


**House of Changes**

My body is a wide house
a commune
of bickering women, hearing
their own breathing
denying each other.

Nearest the door
ready in her black leather
is *Vulnerable*. She lives in the hall
her face painted with care

her black boots reaching her crotch
her black hair shining
her skin milky and soft as butter.
If you should ring the doorbell
she would answer
and a wound would open across her eyes
as she touched your hand.

On the stairs, glossy and determined
is *Mindful*. She's the boss, handing out
punishments and rations and examination
papers with precise
justice. She keeps her perceptions in a huge
album under her arm
her debts in the garden with the weedkill
friends in a card-index
on the windowsill of the sittingroom
and a tape-recording of the world
on earphones
which she plays to herself over and over
assessing her life
writing summaries.

In the kitchen is *Commendable*.
The only lady in the house who
dresses in florals
she is always busy, always doing something
for someone she has
a lot of friends. Her hands are quick and
cunning as blackbirds
her pantry is stuffed with loaves and fishes
she knows the times of trains and
mends fuses and makes
a lot of noise with the vacuum cleaner.
In her linen cupboard, new-ironed and neatly
folded, she keeps her resentments like
wedding presents – each week
takes them out for counting not to
lose any but would never think of
using any being a lady.

Upstairs in a white room is
my favourite. She is *Equivocal*
has no flesh on her bones
that are changeable as yarrow stalks.
She hears her green plants talking
watches the bad dreams under the world
unfolding
spends all her days and nights
arranging her symbols
never sleeps
never eats hamburgers
never lets anyone into her room
never asks for anything.

In the basement is *Harmful.*
She is the keeper of weapons
the watchdog. Keeps intruders at bay
but the others keep her
locked up in the daytime and when she escapes
she comes out screaming
smoke streaming from her nostrils
flames on her tongue
razor-blades for fingernails
skewers for eyes.

I am *Imminent*
live out in the street
watching them. I lodge myself in other people's
heads with a sleeping bag
strapped to my back.
One day I'll perhaps get to like them enough
those rough, truthful women
to move in. One by one
I'm making friends with them all
unobtrusively, slow and steady
slow and steady.

## I and Wolverine

From the tundras of the north you have come
into my belly
and my body is stiff with ice, dangerous
wasted in arctic darkness and my subsoil is frozen.
I know you hunger, I name you Gulo Gulo –
Come forth out of my body.

*I am not what I seem. Passing through me*
*all the starving weasels of the world*
*bristling, red-eyed, hunt their last meal*
*howl their last word, smell their last moon.*
*It hungers me, it hungers me.*

Yet I have seen you leaping on Elk and Reindeer
six feet long, sinking your teeth in the jugular
vein, devouring them, blood and flesh and bone
cloven hoof and antler and furred skin
and still you are hungry. Voracious one
I name you Wolverine
and bind you now to silence in my body –
Be still.

*Yet it hungers me. Once two hundred cubs, new born*
*yellow striped on face and flank, plaster on their skulls*
*and needles in their foreheads*
*drank from a glass beaker, drop by drop*
*sleeping in rows on concrete slabs, making no sound.*

Babies. They were human babies
in a hospital called Baragwanath. I saw them I
told you about them. Doctors were feeding them
vitamins and proteins into the blood were
saving them.
They weren't even awake, they couldn't
feel any hunger. It was long ago.

*It hungers me. A weasel once, blind and young*
*covered in sores, starving*
*strayed into a city. He stood before me*
*jabbing at his open mouth*
*with his paw. I had nothing to give him.*

A man. He was a man. I gave him two shillings.
How you lie and distort everything.
You inhabit me like a madman with your stories
demanding and threatening. You rattle in me
like a sack of empty cans, you grapple and writhe.
I will have you prised from my gut
like a tape-worm, I will have you
exorcised. Malevolent spirit I
recognise you, Carcajou I name you —
Be gone from my body.

*Once long ago in the frozen north*
*the ice melted into milk. It poured forth in warm*
*rivers it lapped and rocked in the sea bed.*
*How I swam then sweetly as a dolphin.*
*Ah it hungers me still, it hungers me.*

Insatiable one, I'm exhausted with eating
I'm a bag of stones, I am all stomach. Bloated
I lie here unable to move in my sea of flesh.
My thighs and breasts flow without shape
my head sags in a heap of chins
I lie here defiled in a mound of
self-disgust, in a pool of half-digested fluids
yet you hunger and hunger in me.
I was a woman once.

*I too. I was human once. Child in a white dress*
*wearing ribbons. There were pansies in the garden*
*with angry faces. They were purple bright*
*O they were furious.*

How you lie. You lie and lie
grinding your canines. You are Wolverine
your snout covered in blood, your hot side
panting. You were born in a forest in the north
tearing flesh from the soft throat of life

quick and invisible and savage
always ravenous as you are now
voracious you stalk your prey without ever resting
leaping in the dark, sniffing wind.

## The Way Towards Each Other

The way towards each other is through our bodies.
Words are the longest distance you can travel
so complex and hazardous you
lose your direction.

Time is no way either. A river mouth it opens
to a mixing of waters, a tidal
diffusion, never
a consummation.

In our bodies we are fallen in a thorn thicket.
Out is a tearing apart, a letting of juices.
Inside though is a pathway, a tremulous compensation —
the possibility of touching.


## The Way Out

The way out is through fire,
a burning stairway
three doors like sentries.

The last but one
child from another time
steadies herself to brave it

then slight and calm
darts into the burning.
Her courage cannot save her —

a haze of blue flames etch
their mad dance
that draws her like wind

waves of heat curl hissing
and scarlet break on her calves
she cries out with pain

as she passes through the first door
and labours upward
where soundless as the sun

the white fire
folds her to its breast.
Her breath sighs from her now

like dying leaves
as scorched and fainting she meets
the second door heavy as a vault

and passes through it
and climbs unfaltering
into the dark invisible heart of fire.

The last door
glows with angel heat, molten
immovable.

She flings her frail weight
against it
as it bites away her hands.

I remember a bird, nest aflame
its wings alight
circling higher and higher

into a black tar of smoke
like a beating star
circling and rising as its light

grew brighter and unbearably
brighter
towards a doorway that must open

a hand cool as rain
outstretch
at the height of heaven.

The way out is never so bitter
never so bitter.
Perhaps it is through water.

## Transformation

I see you dart into the world
pearly pink like the inside of a shell
streaked with silver.

Look! Look!
I am shouting with joy, rising up
like a phoenix from my pain

With my eyes I behold you
In the flesh I behold you

So a holy man waking into death
from a life of devotion or
martyrdom in flames

might look into the shining face of god
and see at once
he had never believed.

I see you with my eyes
I see you in glory.

From a tatter of flesh I watch them work.
From a pinnacle of joy.
The placenta, purplish liver meat

sails out of my body like a whale
rubbery hands turn it inside out
hold it up to the light.

The sinewy pulsing cord.
In a haze of peace they cut and stitch
my threaded body like scarlet linen

the midwife chatting comfortably
seated at her work, the needle threaded,
the thimble, the green thread

in and out, in and out.
Then washed and trim in clean sheets
they leave us: mother father child

three folded together.
I see your sleeping face
eyelids crescent lines, lips curled translucent

in stillness like a cowrie shell
whirlpool of your hair. I see you breathe.
In a still pool the moon lies quiet.


**Dawn**


Of your hand I could say this
a bird poised mid-air in flight
as delicate and smooth.

Of your mouth
a foxglove in its taking
without edges or hurt.

This of your ear
a tiny sea-horse, immortal
sporting in white waves

and of your eye
a place where no one could hide
nothing lurk.

Of your cupped flesh
smooth in my palm
an agate on the sea-shore

of your back and belly
that they command kisses.
And of your feet I would say

they are inquisitive and gay
as squirrels or birds
and so return to your hand

and begin my voyage
around your loveliness
again and yet again

as in my arms you lie sleeping.

## *From* **A Death in Winter**

Beside the exit, seated at a table
is a grey clerk with a ledger.
At his feet is a kind of box —
a trunk perhaps, a hope chest or
a rubbish bin.

Cross-legged in the doorway
my friend sits, watching light
stream in through the opening.
It soaks her in beauty.

She has given back her future.
In character, neatly folded, she placed it
carefully in the box
and the clerk ticked it off.

Now she takes off her feet, like shoes
gently, one beside the other;
she takes her speech and returns it
syllable by syllable
she unpicks it thoughtfully, like knitting
unravels it, one plain, one purl
meaning by meaning;
she gives back her hands —
lays them down in the box with a smile.
There is no regret in her.
She knows their excellence.
And now she gives back continence, choices,
understanding the strange
comings and goings about her.
Everything she returns is fine and cared for.
The clerk ticks it all off in his ledger.

She is hardly human now
she is almost entirely love
she has given back her children
and very little of the personal
is left in her heart.

To the left of the doorway is a linen basket.
A plump girl, laughing, kneels beside it.
She is handing out gifts
to the souls who come trooping
in through the opening like sunlight.

Hands to grip a finger
feet to walk
the first smile
Mama, Papa, I want, I think
all the trappings of the journey.

My friend smiles across at the girl
as if she were a daughter.

The radiance streams in and over her
soon she will take off the last of her body
and step out
into the stillness.

# Analysis

Word order
line length
Descriptive focus
Sound patterns
ie assonance
alliteration
rhythm
rhyme

repetitions.
Use of space to creat
tensions around words
pace, way of play
with sounds.
Interrelationship
between stanzas.

# Acknowledgements

Thanks are due to the copyright holders of the following poems for permission to publish them in this anthology:

**Stevie Smith:** for 'Major Macroo' from *A Good Time Was Had By All* (1937); for 'Brickenden, Hertfordshire' from *Tender Only to One* (1938); for 'I rode with my darling . . .', 'Touch and Go', 'Man is a Spirit' and 'The River God', from *Harold's Leap* (1950); for 'In the Park' from *Not Waving but Drowning* (1957); for 'The Frog Prince', 'The Small Lady' and 'To Carry the Child', from *The Frog Prince and Other Poems* (1966); for 'Scorpion' from *Scorpion and Other Poems* (1971): copyright © Stevie Smith 1937, 1938, 1950, 1957, 1966, 1971, 1975. All poems and extracts reprinted from *The Collected Poems of Stevie Smith* (Allen Lane, 1975) by permission of James MacGibbon. For 'My Muse' and 'What Poems Are Made Of' from *Me Again: Uncollected Writings of Stevie Smith*, edited by Jack Barbera and William McBrien (Virago Press, 1981): copyright © James MacGibbon 1960, 1969, 1981. Reprinted by permission of James MacGibbon.

**Kathleen Raine:** for 'Self' from *The Pythoness* (1948); for 'Amo Ergo Sum' and 'The Mirage' from *The Year One* (1952); for 'Night Sky' and 'Scala Coeli' from *The Hollow Hill* (1964); for 'Heirloom', '"I felt under my old breasts, this April day"', 'The Dead' and '"Long ago I thought you young, bright daimon"', from *The Lost Country* (1971); for the extracts from *On a Deserted Shore* (1973); for 'Turner's Seas' from *The Oval Portrait* (1977); for '"Behind the lids of sleep"' from *The Oracle in the Heart* (1978): copyright © Kathleen Raine 1981. All reprinted from *Collected Poems 1935-1980* by permission of the author and George Allen & Unwin (Publishers) Ltd.

**Denise Levertov:** for 'The Jacob's Ladder' from *The Jacob's Ladder* (1961); for 'The Ache of Marriage' from *O Taste and See* (1964); for 'The Mutes', 'Life at War' and 'Living', from *The Sorrow Dance* (1967): all from *Poems 1960-1967* (1983), published by New Directions Publishing Corporation. For 'A Tree Telling of Orpheus' from *Relearning the Alphabet* (1970); for 'The Sun Going Down upon Our Wrath' from *Footprints* (1972); for 'Fragrance of Life, Odor of Death' from *The Freeing of the Dust* (1975); for 'Death Psalm: O Lord of Mysteries' from *Life in the Forest* (1978); for 'Talk in the Dark' from *Candles in Babylon* (1982): all books published by New Directions Publishing Corporation. Copyright © Denise Levertov 1961, 1964, 1967, 1970, 1972, 1975, 1978, 1982, 1985. All reprinted from *Selected Poems* (Bloodaxe Books, 1985) by permission of the author and New Directions Publishing Corporation. For 'The Task', 'St Peter and the Angel' and '. . . That Passeth All Understanding', from *Oblique Prayers* (New Directions, 1984; Bloodaxe Books, 1985): copyright © Denise Levertov 1984, 1985. Reprinted by permission of the author, New Directions Publishing Corporation and Bloodaxe Books Ltd.

**Elizabeth Jennings:** for 'Fantasy' from *Poems*; for 'For a Child Born Dead' from *A Way of Looking*; for 'The Animals' Arrival' and 'A Letter to Peter Levi' from *The Animals' Arrival*: copyright © Elizabeth Jennings 1953, 1955, 1969, 1979. All reprinted from *Selected Poems* (Carcanet, 1979) by permission of David Higham Associates Ltd. For 'In a Garden' and 'Rembrandt's Late Self-Portraits' from *Growing Points*; for 'Almost Drowning', 'Invocation and Incantation', 'Fragment for the Dark', 'Star Midnight', 'A Child in the Night', 'Hatching' and 'Instinct for Seasons', from *Consequently I Rejoice*; for 'Spell of the Elements' and 'A Chorus' from *Moments of Grace*; for 'For a Gentle Friend', 'Is It Dual-Natured' and 'The One Drawback', from *Celebrations and Elegies*: copyright © Elizabeth Jennings 1975, 1977, 1979, 1982. All reprinted from books published by Carcanet New Press Ltd by permission of David Higham Associates Ltd.

**Elaine Feinstein:** for 'Calliope in the labour ward', 'Song of Power', 'Anniversary', 'By the Cam', 'Patience', 'Marriage', 'Dad', 'Coastline', 'At the edge', 'Night thoughts', 'The Medium' and 'Sybil', from *Some Unease and Angels: Selected Poems*: copyright © Elaine Feinstein 1977. Reprinted by permission of Hutchinson Publishing Group Ltd. For the two extracts from *The Feast of Eurydice*, published by Next Editions: copyright © Elaine Feinstein 1980. Reprinted by permission of the author.

**Ruth Fainlight:** for 'Lilith' from *The Region's Violence*; for 'The Other' and 'Definition' from *Another Full Moon*; for 'Stubborn', 'The Prism', 'Here' and 'The Future', from *Fifteen to Infinity*: copyright © Ruth Fainlight 1973, 1976, 1983. Reprinted by permission of Hutchinson Publishing Group Ltd. For 'Introspection of a Sibyl' and 'It Must' from *Sibyls and Others*, published by Hutchinson: copyright © Ruth Fainlight 1980. Reprinted by permission of Tessa Sayle Agency. For 'Gloria' from *To See the Matter Clearly*, published by Macmillan: copyright © Ruth Fainlight 1968. Reprinted by permission of the author. For 'Anticipated' from *Climates*: copyright © Ruth Fainlight 1983. Reprinted by permission of Bloodaxe Books Ltd.

**Sylvia Plath:** for 'Zoo Keeper's Wife', 'Event', 'Ariel', 'Nick and the Candlestick', 'The Night Dances', 'Poppies in October', 'Fever 103°', 'The Applicant', 'Death & Co.' and 'Edge', from *Ariel* (Faber & Faber) and *Crossing the Water* (Faber & Faber): copyright © Ted Hughes 1965, 1971. All reprinted from *Sylvia Plath: Collected Poems* (Faber & Faber, 1981) by permission of Olwyn Hughes. For the extracts from 'A Comparison' and 'Ocean 1212-W' from *Johnny Panic and the Bible of Dreams* (Faber & Faber, 1977): copyright © Ted Hughes 1977. Reprinted by permission of Olwyn Hughes.

**Jenny Joseph:** for 'Rose in the afternoon', 'Dawn walkers', 'Women at Streatham Hill' and 'Warning', from *Rose in the Afternoon* (Dent); for the extract from 'Altarpiece' from *The Thinking Heart* (Secker & Warburg): copyright © Jenny Joseph 1974, 1978. All reprinted by permission of the author. For 'Another old tale', 'In memory of God' and 'The inland sea', from *Beyond Descartes*: copyright © Jenny Joseph 1983. Reprinted by permission of Secker & Warburg Ltd. For the two extracts from *Persephone*: copyright © Jenny Joseph 1985. Reprinted by permission of Bloodaxe Books Ltd.

**Anne Stevenson:** for 'The Victory' and 'The Mother', from *Reversals* (Wesleyan University Press): copyright © Anne Stevenson 1969. Reprinted by permission of the author. For 'Generations' from *Travelling Behind Glass*; for 'After the End of It' from *Enough of Green*; for 'Transparencies', 'The Garden', 'Sonnets for Five Seasons', 'Green Mountain, Black

Mountain' (extract), 'Swifts', 'Buzzard and Alder' and 'Small Philosophical Poem', from *Minute by Glass Minute*: copyright © Anne Stevenson 1974, 1977, 1982. Reprinted by permission of Oxford University Press.

**Fleur Adcock:** for 'Stewart Island', 'Kilpeck', 'Things', 'Below Loughrigg', 'Madmen', 'Blue Glass', 'Instructions to Vampires', and 'Mary Magdalene and the Birds', from *Selected Poems*: copyright © Fleur Adcock 1983. Reprinted by permission of Oxford University Press.

**Jeni Couzyn:** for 'Christmas in Africa' (extract), 'House of Changes', 'I and Wolverine', 'The Way Towards Each Other', 'The Way Out', 'Transformation', 'Dawn' and 'Death in Winter' (extract), from *Life by Drowning: Selected Poems*, published by Bloodaxe Books Ltd: copyright © Jeni Couzyn 1983, 1985. Reprinted by permission of Curtis Brown.

The prose quotations in the essay 'Stevie Smith' by Jeni Couzyn are from: *Ivy and Stevie: Ivy Compton-Burnett and Stevie Smith, Conversations and Reflections* by Kay Dick (Duckworth, 1971; Allison & Busby, 1983); and *The Holiday* by Stevie Smith (Chapman and Hall, 1949; Virago, 1979). The poem 'For My Lover Returning to His Wife' by Anne Sexton quoted in the introduction is from *Anne Sexton: Complete Poems* (Houghton Mifflin, 1984).

The photograph of Sylvia Plath with her children and mother on page 145 is reprinted by permission of Faber & Faber Ltd from *Letters Home* by Sylvia Plath, edited by Aurelia Schober Plath (Faber & Faber, 1976).

Thanks are also due to the following for photographs of the poets: Stevie Smith, page 31 (Penguin Books Ltd) and 32 (National Portrait Gallery); Kathleen Raine, page 55 (Tara Heinemann) and 56 (Peter Milroy); Denise Levertov, pages 73 and 74 (David Geier); Elizabeth Jennings, pages 97 and 98 (Peter Milroy); Elaine Feinstein, pages 112 and 113 (Peter Milroy); Ruth Fainlight, pages 128 (D. Sillitoe) and 129 (T. Hulf); Sylvia Plath, page 144 (Rollie McKenna); Jenny Joseph, pages 165 (Stuart Redler) and 166 (Tara Heinemann); Anne Stevenson, pages 183 (Peter Milroy) and 184 (Susan Butler); Fleur Adcock, pages 199 (Jane Ussher) and 200 (Marti Friedlander); and Jeni Couzyn, pages 213 (Colin Marr) and 214 (Simon Thirsk).

JACQUELINE MORREAU

Jacqueline Morreau was educated in California and moved to London in 1972. She co-organised the exhibition 'Women's Images of Men' at the ICA in 1980, and is contributing editor of a book called *Women's Images of Men* (Writers & Readers, 1984) which takes up issues raised by the exhibition.

In her own work she explores politics, feminism and the subject of woman as artist. Her paintings and drawings have been widely exhibited, and her commissions from publishers have included book covers for the Women's Press, Brilliance Books, and for Jeni Couzyn's *Life by Drowning: Selected Poems* (Bloodaxe Books, 1985). A book of her work will be published in 1985 by Scarecrow Press, New Jersey.

Her cover painting for *The Bloodaxe Book of Contemporary Women Poets* is 'She Who Weaves' (1984), oil on board, 40" x 39".

# Index of Titles and First Lines